FUNDAMENTALS OF ARTIFICIAL INTELLIGENCE & LARGE LANGUAGE MODELS

MASTER PROMPT ENGINEERING AND MONETIZE THE POWER OF LANGUAGE PROCESSING

RUSSELL DAWSON

TABLE OF CONTENTS

INTRODUCTION

Since the introduction of ChatGPT, in 2022, the world has undergone a significant technological transformation. This has resulted in artificial intelligence (AI) and large language models (LLMs) becoming popular and a constant in our lives. In 2025, AI is not just a technological advancement—it is a force reshaping our daily lives, businesses, and society at an unprecedented pace.

According to the "Stanford AI Index Report (2024)," over 80% of Fortune 500 companies now integrate AI into their operations, while 97% of mobile users already interact with AI-powered applications daily (*The State of AI*, 2024). The global AI market, valued at approximately $380 billion in 2022, is projected to reach $1.3 trillion by 2029 (*51 Artificial Intelligence Statistics*, 2024). These numbers reflect the technology's explosive growth and adoption across industries.

The effects of this revolution can be seen in almost every industry. In healthcare, AI algorithms now detect diseases with accuracy, rivaling human specialists. Financial institutions use AI to process millions of transactions while detecting fraud in real time. Education systems employ adaptive learning platforms that can personalize the content for each student. Even creative industries have embraced AI, with tools that assist in content creation, design, and music composition.

At the same time, this impact extends beyond large corporations. Small businesses and entrepreneurs are increasingly leveraging AI tools for customer service, marketing optimization, and operational efficiency. Studies show that companies implementing AI solutions report an average 25% increase in operational efficiency and a 20% reduction in operational costs (Matleena S & Brian, 2024). Still, according to the report, the impact of AI in business is set to increase, with 20% of the tech budget being allocated to AI and 58% of the companies looking to increase their investments in the technology.

If these statistics and technical terms seem overwhelming, don't worry. You are not alone. Many people find AI and LLMs intimidating at first glance. That is precisely why this book was written: to help demystify these technologies through clear and practical explanations you can understand, as well as to show how AI can help you with real-world examples. Whether you are a business professional, student, or simply curious about AI, this guide will help you understand how to harness these powerful tools.

By reading this book, you will

- have a clear understanding of AI fundamentals and how LLMs work
- obtain the practical knowledge to evaluate and implement AI solutions
- gather insights on AI's potential impact on diverse fields
- harness the skills to stay competitive in an AI-driven world
- gain confidence in discussing and working with AI technologies

Think about it this way: The AI revolution is not slowing down, quite the contrary—it's accelerating. Companies are looking to invest more in AI, and researchers are increasing their efforts to make it more powerful. Things are constantly changing, and you will miss out on the latest developments. At the same time, by understanding these technologies now, you're not just learning for the future but also preparing to be an active participant in shaping it.

As you get ready to start this discovery adventure into the world of AI and LLMs, rest assured that by the end of the book, you will have all the foundational knowledge to build upon. The future is AI-powered, and this book is your guide to understanding and thriving in it. If you are ready to see the world as many do today, get your computer to explore as we go and find a comfortable place to sit. You are about to start a learning experience that will forever change how you see the world and interact with technology. Shall we begin?

INTRODUCTION TO AI

W henever your smartphone recognizes your face, your junk mail is separated from what really matters, or you receive that perfect recommendation for a movie night, that is AI at work. These everyday experiences and most of our interactions with technology today are powered by these intelligent systems. As you read this, AI systems are diagnosing diseases, driving cars, trading stocks, and even creating art and music. But what exactly makes these systems *intelligent?* What characteristics make machines able to work similar to how a human does?

In this chapter, we will decode the fundamental concepts of AI, moving beyond the buzzwords and jargon to understand how it actually works. For example, did you know that there is more than one type of AI? As you read, you will explore its different types, from simple rule-based programs to sophisticated neural networks, and examine how machine learning (ML) and deep learning (DL) revolutionized what computers can do. As you explore this technology and its applications, you will gain a broader understanding of how AI already plays a major role in our lives, from healthcare to transportation and entertainment, and learn to distinguish between AI fact and fiction.

Whether you are a business professional looking to implement AI solutions or simply curious about this incredible technology, you will find the information you need to build the foundation to understand why AI is considered the next Industrial Revolution.

WHAT IS AI?

AI represents humans' attempt to make machines think like them. In other words, it is the idea of recreating the human thought process in machines so that they can function as a human would. AI is a branch of computer science that is focused on building smart machines that carry out the most varied tasks, such as recognizing speech, making decisions, and understanding patterns. While these abilities were usually understood to be exclusive to the human mind, AI came to change this.

The concept of AI emerged in Ancient Greece when philosophers discussed the ability of objects that could think. Much closer to the present, in the 1950s, computer scientist Alan Turing proposed the Turing Test to determine if a machine could exhibit intelligent behavior that could not be distinguished from a human. This sparked a scientific revolution that continues today. While early AI systems were simple rule-based programs, that would function according to a set of preestablished parameters, modern AI has evolved into sophisticated systems that can learn from new experiences and adapt to new situations.

The main idea behind AI development is not just to replicate human intelligence but also to enhance and extend our capabilities. Today's AI systems excel at processing vast amounts of data, recognizing complex patterns, and making fast decisions, areas in which humans still have limitations. One example of this application is in medicine, since while a human radiologist might analyze dozens of medical images per day, an AI system can process thousands, thus supporting (not replacing) medical professionals in their diagnostic work.

But what sets AI apart from other computer systems? That is a good question. The main difference between a simple computer program and an AI application is the latter's ability to learn and improve from experience. While conventional software follows fixed rules, AI systems can adjust their behavior based on new data and outcomes. This adaptability makes AI particularly valuable for tasks where rules are difficult to explicitly define or where conditions frequently change.

This is the incredible magic of modern AI: It achieves these capabilities through multiple approaches ranging from basic statistical analysis to complex neural networks that mimic the human brain's structure, which you will learn more about further along in the chapter. These systems process information through layers of interconnected nodes, each contributing to the final output, regardless of the task.

But let's not get ahead of ourselves. The first thing you should understand is AI's fundamental nature, which helps explain its transformative impact across industries. AI is not just a tool for automation; it's a technology that augments human intelligence, enabling us to solve previously unsolvable problems and discover new possibilities. To start off, let's understand the different types of AI and how they are used today.

TYPES OF AI

Understanding the differences between AI systems can be confusing at times. To make it easier, you should think about these systems based on two general classifications: capability- and functionality-based AI. Let's see what each of them are and how they differ.

Capability-Based AI

These refer to what the AI system can *do*. It is divided into three subcategories: narrow or weak AI (artificial narrow intelligence [ANI]), general or strong AI (artificial general intelligence [AGI]), and artificial superintelligence (ASI). Here is a breakdown with a description and examples of each:

- **ANI:** Excels at specific tasks while lacking a broader understanding. This is the case when you unlock your phone with face recognition. When this happens, the system can perfectly recognize your features but knows nothing about your identity or preferences. Similarly, when you play chess against a computer, it might make masterful moves but cannot transfer that strategic thinking to another game or engage in conversation about its choices. These systems, despite their limitations, power much of the technology we use today. Think about how spam filters protect your email inbox—they are remarkably effective at identifying unwanted messages but cannot understand their content or context.
- **AGI:** AI systems might seem versatile, but they are actually combining multiple narrow AI systems. On the other hand, with AGI, you would be able to have a conversation with the computer about philosophy or ask it to help you solve complex mathematical equations. They are so versatile that they can compose music and design buildings, all while understanding their interconnection. In this case, AGI would match human-level intelligence across all cognitive domains, learning and adapting like a human mind. At the same time, systems such as these do not yet exist but are currently in development. Think of C-3PO from *Star Wars*: a machine that can truly understand context, independently learn new skills, and engage in genuine humanlike reasoning.
- **ASI:** This technology represents intelligence that would surpass human capabilities in every conceivable way. This

means it could be a system that could solve climate change while simultaneously discovering new physics principles and revolutionizing healthcare—all in a couple of days or hours. While this might sound like a science fiction movie, it represents the ultimate potential and risks of AI development. Systems such as these would process information faster than the entire human population combined while demonstrating creativity and insight beyond our comprehension.

Functionality-Based AI

These refer to how AI systems process information and make decisions. They are categorized on their ability to handle data, learn, and interact with their environment. They are broken down into the following four categories:

- **Reactive AI:** Think about a traffic light system that adjusts the signal timing based on current traffic flow. It does not remember past traffic patterns or learn over time; it simply reacts to present conditions. This is reactive AI and the most popular example is IBM's Deep Blue chess computer, the first of its kind. This computer operated similarly, analyzing each board position fresh without referring to past games or learning from experience. While they might seem like limited technology, these systems are highly skilled performers who perfectly execute their tasks but cannot explain their methods or adapt to new situations.
- **Limited memory AI:** An easily identifiable example of this type of AI may be lying in the palm of your hand. This is because your phone's navigation app is one of the most relatable examples of the technology. It does not just react to current traffic conditions but learns from historical data patterns and your previous routes to suggest better paths. Modern self-driving cars can take this further, combining real-time sensor data with learned experience about how

other vehicles behave, weather conditions affecting driving, and how to navigate complex intersections. These systems demonstrate how AI can use past experiences to make better present decisions.

- **Theory of mind AI:** These systems are purely theoretical, but it would be similar to having a healthcare robot that can monitor vital signs and recognize when the patient feels anxious. When this happens, it would be able to adjust its communication style accordingly and build rapport over time. This type of technology still hasn't been achieved, but some social robots being worked on by developers are taking steps in this direction. To make them fully functional, the system would need to understand that humans have thoughts and emotions that influence their behavior, capabilities crucial for meaningful human–AI interaction.

- **Self-aware AI:** The most advanced theoretical type of AI would be a system that is self-conscious and has awareness comparable to humans. This would be like the AI from the movie *Her*, a system that thinks, feels, and understands its own existence, forming genuine emotional connections. Technology such as this is still only in the speculation field and helps raise questions and debates on the nature of consciousness in humans itself.

Understanding these AIs allows you to identify the type of technology you are dealing with. While most applications today use narrow, reactive, or limited memory AI, the field continues to rapidly evolve. This evolution is largely driven by advances in ML and DL, powerful approaches that enable AI systems to improve through experience. In the next section, we will explore how these learning technologies work and why they have become the force behind the most impressive achievements in the industry.

MACHINE LEARNING AND DEEP LEARNING

To understand modern AI's capabilities, it is essential to explore two key technologies that power most of these applications: ML and DL. These approaches have revolutionized how computers learn and solve problems, moving beyond traditional programming systems that can improve through experience.

Machine Learning: Teaching Computers to Learn

Suppose you want to teach a child to recognize cats. Instead of listing every feature of the animal, such as whiskers, pointy ears, and fur, you would show them many pictures of cats until they can learn to identify one on their own. ML works similarly. Rather than programming explicit rules, the computer is fed large amounts of data and lets them discover patterns.

Let's use the email spam filter again as an example. Traditional programming would require manually writing rules that would identify the messages as spam. ML instead analyzes millions of emails marked as spam or not spam, learning to identify patterns that humans might not even notice. Over time, this system improves as it sees more examples, just as a person would get better at spotting spam with experience.

This approach transformed many applications we use today. Netflix, for example, recommends shows based on viewing patterns, virtual assistants understand different accents by learning from millions of samples, and fraud detection systems protect our credit cards by learning what suspicious transactions look like. In Chapter 3, you will learn more about how these learning processes take place and their different types. In the meantime, read on to discover what DL is and how it takes ML to the next level.

Deep Learning: Inspired by the Human Brain

DL takes ML further by mimicking how our brains process information. Just as our brains use neuron networks to understand complex patterns, DL uses artificial neural networks with multiple layers to solve increasingly sophisticated problems. This layered approach enabled breakthroughs in areas that were previously challenging for computers. Language translation, for example, now captures subtle context and meaning, medical imaging systems detect diseases with remarkable accuracy, and autonomous vehicles can interpret complex road situations in real time.

Consider how you recognize a friend's face. Your brain does not consciously think *oval face, brown eyes,* or *curved nose.* It simultaneously processes all these features through neuron layers. DL systems work similarly, breaking down complex tasks into layers of similar patterns. When identifying objects in photos, early layers might detect basic edges and shapes, middle layers combine these into features like eyes or wheels, and deep layers assemble these features into complete objects like faces or cars.

While these are the basic concepts of ML and DL, you will learn more about how this learning process takes place further into the book, gaining insight into how they learn and improve. In them, you will explore the training process, different learning approaches, and how these systems handle new situations. For now, let's look into areas in which AI is currently making a significant impact, affecting different industries and aspects of our lives.

WHERE IS AI USED TODAY?

So far, you have seen how AI is being used in email spam filters, streaming services, voice assistants, and even self-driving cars. However, AI has evolved well beyond these applications. While the previously seen examples have become everyday conveniences, their influence stretches much further, quietly transforming industries in ways that many people are unaware of. From agriculture to law enforcement, AI is enhancing decision-making, improving efficiency, and unlocking new possibilities. Read on to discover what they are.

- **Agriculture:** AI is being used in agriculture with precision farming techniques that improve yields while reducing waste. Smart drones and sensors collect real-time data on soil health, weather conditions, and crop growth. Advanced AI algorithms analyze this data to recommend optimal planting, fertilization, and irrigation schedules. Additionally, these systems are used to monitor livestock health by tracking behavior patterns and detecting early illness signs.
- **Fashion:** By analyzing vast datasets of consumer preferences, social media activity, and cultural shifts, AI is being used to forecast future trends that can impact the industry. Companies are also using the technology to create custom clothing designs tailored to individual body measurements, preferences, and sustainability criteria. AI-driven virtual try-ons are enhancing online shopping experiences by helping customers visualize how garments and makeup will look before purchasing.
- **Art conservation and restoration:** AI has become an essential tool in aiding in the preservation of cultural heritage by analyzing artwork and detecting deterioration that may not be visible to the human eye. ML models can predict material degradation over time and suggest conservation strategies. In some cases, the technology has been used to digitally restore damaged or incomplete art pieces, offering a glimpse into lost masterpieces.
- **Wildlife conservation:** Organizations and governments are currently deploying AI in wildlife reserves to prevent poaching. Cameras and sensors equipped with AI algorithms can detect human presence in restricted areas and alert park rangers in real time. These systems can also be used to track

and study animal populations, helping researchers monitor endangered species and their habitats.

- **Journalism:** AI technology is being used to assist journalists by generating news summaries and even writing basic articles such as sports scores, financial reports, and weather updates. This allows the journalist to focus on in-depth investigative reporting and complex stories. At the same time, despite AI's growing role, human editorial oversight remains essential to ensure accuracy and ethical reporting.

- **Architecture:** Have you ever imagined living in a house that was designed by AI? Today, this is possible! AI is enabling generative design, where algorithms create thousands of design options based on specific parameters such as space constraints, material usage, and environmental factors. By using it, architects can choose the best designs or refine them further. This approach helps speed up the design process and results in more efficient and sustainable structures.

- **Entertainment:** In this industry, AI is used to assist with scriptwriting by generating plot ideas, dialogue, and character development suggestions. While these tools can help writers overcome creative blocks, the final script always requires a human touch to ensure depth, originality, and emotional connection. It is also being used to create background scenarios and help filmmakers create more realistic special effects.

- **Legal:** This sector is using AI to automate tedious tasks such as contract review and conducting due diligence during mergers and acquisitions. When correctly employed, it can quickly identify potential risks, flag unusual clauses, and ensure compliance with regulations. At the same time, as with many of the other industries, it is essential to have lawyers or paralegals review the work to interpret complex legal nuances and make judgment calls.

- **Logistics:** AI technology is fueling transportation platforms to help optimize delivery routes by analyzing traffic patterns, weather conditions, and road closures. This helps reduce delivery times and lowers fuel consumption and operational costs. To take it even further, AI can predict vehicle maintenance needs, preventing costly breakdowns and delays.

- **Mental health:** While AI can be used as a virtual therapist to provide support for people with anxiety, depression, and stress 24/7, this is a use that needs caution. Access to mental health resources and guidance on cognitive behavioral therapy exercises are a few of its benefits. At the same time, while helpful, they are designed to complement, not replace, human therapists.

- **Mining:** To ensure that mining activities are safer and operations are enhanced, AI is employed in the industry to predict equipment failures before they occur and monitor working conditions for potential hazards. By analyzing data from sensors embedded in the machinery, AI helps reduce downtime and prevent accidents.

- **Retail:** If you have ever noticed the increase or decrease of a product's price on a website, you are experiencing AI use first-hand. Retailers are using the technology to implement dynamic pricing models that adjust product prices in real time based on factors such as demand, competition, and customer behavior. This ensures optimal pricing strategies that maximize sales and profit margins.

- **Forensics:** AI is being used in forensic science to reconstruct crime scenes using data from evidence collected on-site. ML models can simulate scenarios and provide insights that help investigators piece together what happened. Finally, the use of technology allows investigations to be faster and more accurate.

- **Marine biology:** Underwater drones are being used to map the ocean floor with greater precision than ever before. These systems also collect data on marine life, underwater ecosystems, and geological features, aiding in environmental research and conservation efforts.

- **Education:** This is another area that is being greatly transformed by AI. In education, AI is transforming teaching by creating personalized learning experiences tailored to each student's pace, strengths, and weaknesses. Intelligent tutoring systems can adapt content based on real-time performance, helping students grasp difficult concepts more effectively.

The examples you have seen show the vast and surprising ways AI is being used today. From protecting wildlife to revolutionizing fashion and forensics, it may seem that AI's potential is limitless. However, it is essential to remember that while AI can automate and enhance many tasks, it still requires human oversight. Ethical considerations, critical thinking, and empathy are elements that only human beings can provide. As you continue to learn about AI, it is crucial to identify the right balance between AI-driven automation and human intervention.

And where do tools like ChatGPT come in? This is an excellent question that you will start to explore in the next chapter. In it, you will learn more about LLMs, the technology behind the most popular models used today. Get ready to see how these models work, what makes them different from other AI types, and how they are trained to generate humanlike language.

UNDERSTANDING LARGE LANGUAGE MODELS

When ChatGPT burst onto the scene in 2022, it sparked a global conversation about AI and its capabilities. The tool uses a technology known as LLMs, which are sophisticated AI systems that can understand and generate humanlike text. These models transformed how we interact with computers, making it possible to have natural conversations with machines, generate creative content, and solve complex problems using simple dialogue.

In this chapter, you will learn more about LLMs and explore why they represent such a significant leap forward in AI technology. You will learn what makes these systems different from traditional AI, understand its key components, and discover how they are reshaping industries in the market. With the information you are about to see, you will have the essential knowledge to understand and later use and engage in the LLM revolution.

WHAT ARE LLMS?

Imagine you have an assistant at work who has read most of the text available on the internet and can talk about almost any subject. This is what an LLM is: an AI system trained on massive amounts of data that can understand and generate humanlike language. The "large" in LLMs refers to the amount of data they are trained on and their complexity. Modern LLM models such as GPT-4 have processed more text than any human could read in multiple lifetimes. This extensive training allows them to understand context, recognize patterns, and generate responses across multiple topics and tasks.

To make it easier, think of an LLM as a superpowered prediction engine for language. When you type in "The weather today is," the model predicts what words might naturally come next. This is a similar feature to what you have on your phone and are typing a text; based on your writing style, habits, and common words, it determines what the next word you will type will be. The difference is that LLMs have a much greater capacity and operate at a much more sophisticated level. This ability comes from analyzing billions of examples of human writing, including books, articles, websites, conversations, and several other sources available on the internet. Some of these sources include

- books and academic papers
- websites and news articles
- social media conversations
- code repositories
- online forums and discussions
- educational materials
- legal documents
- technical documentation

All these are part of the training process that helps LLMs understand different writing styles, topics, and contexts. For example, when you ask an LLM to explain quantum physics, it can adjust its language depending on whether you are a child or a physics student. Similarly, it will cover the topic based on the angle you are looking for and the instructions you give it, which are known as *prompts*. The machine will analyze this information and, based on the feedback it receives and the follow-up questions you ask, will determine the best approach or answer to give you.

Let's use an example of how children learn once again to understand this process. As a child, you did not start to learn how to speak by learning and memorizing grammar rules. You likely learned by listening to others speak, reading books, and gradually picking up patterns. You paid attention to the order in which others spoke their works and mimicked it or were corrected until you got it right. LLMs learn similarly but at a massive scale. They analyze patterns in text: which words often appear together, how sentences are structured, and how ideas connect across paragraphs. When this learning takes place, it allows the machine to

- convert complex technical documents into simple explanations
- answer questions about specific topics
- write creative content
- help with coding
- translate between languages
- summarize long documents
- engage in natural conversations

While LLMs have all these capabilities, one thing that is essential to understand is that these LLMs don't actually "think" like humans do. They are simply a sophisticated pattern recognition system that can generate appropriate responses based on their training. They don't have real-world experience or consciousness; they are simply processing patterns in text data in a sophisticated way. No matter how powerful they are, LLMs are still an example of ANI that you have seen in the previous chapter, as they have an incredible capacity to work with language-related texts but cannot understand or reason like humans. LLMs are a result of the combination of reactive and limited memory machines, responding to current inputs while drawing on their training data. This helps explain their impressive capabilities and limitations.

On the other hand, what sets LLMs apart from other AI systems is their unique approach to processing and generating language. Unlike traditional AI programs that follow strict rules or make simple predictions, LLMs can engage with language in ways that seem remarkably humanlike. This differentiation is essential to have a deeper understanding of its potential and challenges, which we are about to explore next.

HOW ARE LLMS DIFFERENT FROM OTHER AIS?

While traditional AI systems are like highly skilled specialists trained for specific tasks, LLMs are more versatile, like conversation partners. In the first, it would be like a chess master player who can beat opponents but does not know how to explain how or why he did it. In the latter, it is like talking to a friend who can speak multiple languages and adapt to different topics or demonstrate creativity. The second clearly has an incredible advantage over the first.

In real-life applications, traditional AI could be represented in Apple's Face ID, which can only be used to unlock your phone, voice assistants that can only respond to specific commands, or autocorrect, which can only fix spelling mistakes. With LLMs, it would be telling the machine, *Hey, can you write an email to my boss asking about taking tomorrow off because I am feeling ill with the appropriate tone and formatting?* Once this has been entered, the machine would follow the instructions, creating a professional email with an explanation and the correct tone.

This flexibility comes from how LLMs process language. Unlike traditional AI systems that follow predefined rules or decision trees, LLMs understand context and can generate appropriate responses based on the situation. This means, for example, they can adjust the language from a text from casual, to technical or simple, based on the context. With the same application, you can write a professional business email and a playful children's story. These programs can also handle ambiguity and generate creative content, significant advances to the predefined templates other AIs have, giving them the ability to create stories or write poems.

Suppose you are planning on going on vacation. This is how each of these technologies might help you:

Traditional AI	LLMs
Book flights and hotels from a database.	Suggest destinations based on your interests and budget.
Predict weather patterns.	Create a personalized itinerary based on your preferences.
Show restaurant ratings and menus.	Recommend local cuisine and cultural experiences.
Can only convert specific phrases between languages.	Can help you communicate effectively by providing contextual translations.
Send templated messages with prerecorded requests.	Allows you to send and request special requests with personalized messages.

As you can see, LLMs have an incredible versatility that other systems do not have, allowing them to be a powerful ally in carrying out different tasks. At the same time, this versatility comes with its own complexity. To understand how LLMs achieve their capabilities, it is essential to have some comprehension of their key components. In the following section, we will explore the essential elements that make these language models work, from tokenization to attention mechanisms, breaking them down into simple and understandable terms.

UNDERSTANDING KEY COMPONENTS

LLMs are like sophisticated translation systems that can instantly process an incredible amount of information. They create a bridge between human intent and meaningful responses, transforming our simple prompts into coherent and contextual answers. It is like carrying out a search on your browser and receiving a cohesive response without having to read every single article available on the subject.

While these systems may seem magical, they operate through distinct components that work together like instruments in an orchestra. To have a better understanding of this process, read on to see how each of them relates to our everyday tasks, creating answers that seemed previously impossible. As you move through the section, you will see how tokenization, transformers, and attention systems function in collaboration to bring the results you see on the screen.

Tokenization: Breaking Down the Language

Tokenization is to break down the text into small, manageable pieces called tokens. These can be parts of words, full words, or each individual character. In a kitchen, it would be similar to all the ingredients that the chef needs to make a recipe. That will separate each of them and then put them together to make the dish. For example, look at the following phrase:

> *Example:* Let's get ice cream!
> *Tokens:* ["Let's"] ["get"] ["ice"] ["cream"] ["!"]

In this case, the computer would look at every individual word when separating the data. At the same time, some larger words would get broken down into small pieces, such as *overwhelming*, which would be ["over"] ["whelm"] ["ing"]. This process helps the model handle new or uncommon words that it would not usually find in the data it was fed by recognizing familiar parts.

Transformers: The System's Brain

Transformers are the chef who knows how to put all the ingredients together. In this case, they know exactly what work needs to go in each place based on their *experience* and the *knowledge* they have gained over the years. If you read, for example, *The ball flew through the air and smashed the...* you would immediately think *window* because you understand context. Transformers do this by maintaining connections between all words in a sentence.

If you compare this to traditional AI, it would be like a person reading a text with a tiny flashlight, only being able to see a small part at the time. Transformers see everything at once, like reading under a bright light. This allows them to connect related ideas even when far apart, understand context and references, and maintain consistency in long responses.

In this case, if you have ever used ChatGPT or a similar tool and you "continue" a conversation within the same chat, it still recalls what you wrote and can continue the same idea throughout. On the other hand, if you delete the conversation or start a new window, it will not be able to remember it, thus showing one of its vulnerabilities. Transformers are powerful tools, but they can only be used if they have the appropriate context and knowledge to make use of these tokens.

Attention Mechanisms: Focusing on What Matters

Finally, you have the attention mechanisms. To still use our kitchen analogy, it would be the chef knowing what techniques, time, and conditions under which to cook the recipe. In another example, it would be like how your brain works when reading a mystery novel. When you read the phrase "the butler did it," your mind will immediately connect to all the previous mentions of the butler. In LLMs, this attention helps focus on relevant information while generating all responses.

Think about the following example:

> *Example:* John went to Paris because he loves French cuisine.
> *Attention mechanism:* Connects the "he" with "John" and understands that "French cuisine" is related to "Paris."

This is where the magic of AI machines happens since if the cook does not know the correct techniques to apply, the food will be bad. Similarly, if the machine is not appropriately trained or the data is skewed, the answers will be unreliable, since it does not have the proper setup to work. This can lead to information inaccuracies or the inability to identify ambiguity or even false information.

Putting It All Together

When interacting with an LLM, the components you have seen will work in the following sequence:

1. Your input gets tokenized into pieces.
2. Transformers process these tokens, understanding relationships.
3. Attention mechanisms highlight relevant connections.
4. The model generates a response using this understanding.

This process is similar to how data analysts process information, as explained in *Fundamentals of Data Analytics in Today's World: A Comprehensive Guide for Beginners.* Just as they must break down complex datasets, understand relationships between variables, and focus on relevant patterns to draw meaningful conclusions, LLMs process language through structured steps. In our kitchen scenario, here is an overview of the process:

AI technical process	Real-life scenario
Tokenization	Breaking the order into ingredients
Transformers	Understanding how ingredients work together
Attention	Focusing on the right techniques and timing
Output	Creating the final dish

These components enable LLMs to handle complex tasks that were impossible for earlier AI systems. The impact of this technology has been revolutionary across industries and applications, which you will explore in the next section. In it, you will see the transformative power these systems have brought to the market for both good and bad.

THE IMPACT OF LLMS TODAY

In the previous chapter, you saw how AI is generally changing many of the markets in the world. However, this impact is even more significant when considering LLMs, since it has transformed different aspects of our daily lives, influencing how we work, learn, and interact with technology. From assisting in complex research to automating content creation, LLMs are driving a new era of efficiency and creativity. In this final section, you will explore some examples of industries you have seen before, but taking it a step further because they are also using LLMs.

- **Education:** This is one of the sectors that is experiencing the most significant changes due to LLMs. By providing instant and on-demand learning support, LLMs are making education more accessible and personalized than before. Virtual tutors powered by these models help students understand difficult topics, draft essays, and solve math problems. According to *AI in Education Market* (2024), it is estimated that education is the largest revenue share of this market, with 70.3% in 2024, estimated to reach a compound annual growth rate of more than $32 billion by 2030. Today, platforms such as the Khan Academy have integrated LLMs to offer personalized learning according to each student's pace and proficiency.

- **Content creation:** As the precursor among the earliest beneficiaries of LLM technology, content creation has seen a significant change in the industry. Writers, marketers, and designers now use these tools to generate blog posts, social media content, product descriptions, and even video descriptions in a fraction of the time it would take to do manually. Two examples of popular tools are Jasper AI and Copy.ai, which are powered by advanced LLMs that have helped people produce marketing content more efficiently, freeing up creative teams to focus on strategy. According to Khan (2024), 59% of marketers see the potential for AI in content creation, while only 26% agree to use it. At the same time, 71% of these professionals claim that LLMs will help eliminate busy work, allowing them to focus on more strategic tasks.

- **Customer service:** LLMs have substantially impacted customer service, especially when referring to AI-powered chatbots. Several companies have implemented the technology to offer 24/7 assistance, including virtual agents and helpdesk solutions to address customer queries. Doing so has allowed customer demands to be addressed at any time of the day, offering instant responses and reducing wait times. Companies like Zendesk and HubSpot have integrated LLMs into their support systems, enabling 24/7 customer assistance and improving user satisfaction. Implementing these systems has boosted operational efficiency by 25%, with 69% of customers preferring chatbots for communication with their service providers (A. Khan, 2024).

- **Healthcare:** From assisting doctors with medical research to helping patients understand complex diagnoses, LLMs have proven to be an incredible asset for healthcare. These systems can analyze large volumes of medical literature and offer suggestions for treatment plans based on medical best practices. With the implementation of LLMs in the medical industry, professionals have access to an integrated system with information that analyzes different drug combination possibilities. Tools like IBM's Watson and DeepMind's AlphaFold use LLMs to assist researchers in drug discovery and genetic analysis. While AI is not expected to be 100% accurate for these cases, LLM's responses to medical queries achieved a correct diagnostic 71.7% of the time, an incredible achievement for these machines (Kavanagh, 2023).

- **Legal:** LLMs are being leveraged in the legal industry to streamline labor-intensive tasks such as legal research, contract analysis, and document drafting. Using these tools enables companies to quickly swift through massive datasets to find relevant case law and statutes, saving lawyers countless hours. Companies like Casetext and Luminance currently use LLMs to assist legal teams in reviewing contracts and conducting due diligence more efficiently. The application of these tools can reduce up to 40% of the time spent by paralegals and lawyers in research while reducing errors by up to 90% (*Revolutionising the Legal World*, 2022).

- **Retail:** Retailers are currently deploying LLMs to create personalized shopping experiences, from AI-driven product recommendations to automated customer interactions. In this case, the tools analyze product reviews for sentiment analysis and compare them to customer purchases, offering a seamless shopping experience based on preferences. Ecommerce giants such as Amazon and Shopify use this strategy to analyze customer preference and offer tailored product suggestions, increasing sales and boosting profits. Customers are already getting used to this, especially with 70% expecting personalization in their shopping experiences, with 56% of them claiming a personalized experience motivates them to become repeat buyers (*12 Hyper Personalization Statistics*, 2024).

- **Game development:** Lastly, in the gaming industry, LLMs are being used to create content such as dialogue, quests, and even entire storylines. This reduces the workload for developers and enhances the player experience by offering dynamic and personalized narratives. In this case, the most popularly applied LLM is GPT, with OpenAI's model being integrated into experimental game engines to create interactive environments that will give the player a more immersive experience. A recent survey has identified that 49% of developers claim their companies are already using AI to enhance their video games, a number that is set to escalate, with 90% of these companies looking to implement the technology to decrease costs (Merchant, 2024).

While these examples illustrate the potential LLM technology has across industries, their rapid adoption has also brought challenges. On the positive side, these tools enhance productivity, enable person-alization at scale, and reduce operational costs. On the negative, it includes job displacement, data privacy concerns, and ethical dilemmas related to AI misuse. In Chapter 9, we will discuss this use and how to implement best and ethical practices when using these applications.

In the meantime, let's look somewhat deeper into the LLM process by understanding how they learn, giving you a better overview of its potential challenges and opportunities. In the next chapter, you will learn about the LLM training process, from pretraining on massive datasets to fine-tuning for specific applications.

Understanding these concepts will allow you to have a deeper insight into their capabilities and limitations as a preparation to start using them as a tool to make income.

HOW AI AND LLMS LEARN

H ave you ever wondered how LLM tools can discuss the origins of the universe in one moment and write a song in the next? Or how these systems can recognize cats in photos or detect fraudulent transactions? These are good questions that help you understand how these tools work, so take the information they provide with a grain of salt. In this chapter, you will look under the hood of AI and LLM systems to explore the incredible manner in which they learn. From the massive datasets they train on to the fine-tuning that makes them useful for specific tasks, this is not a simple process.

In fact, as you will see, this training process includes parameters and data sources, both of which are a strength and a weakness for LLMs. Understanding how these systems learn is crucial for their best use, especially recognizing potential pitfalls. You will explore why AI sometimes makes mistakes, shows biases, or generates false information, giving you the necessary knowledge to responsibly and efficiently use these tools in your work and daily life.

TRAINING PROCESS

Teaching an AI system is much like training for a specific task or becoming extremely proficient in a subject. However, this process takes place for different tasks and subjects simultaneously, in which it will learn from millions of examples rather than just a few. Regardless of the type of model you are working with, or what you want it to do, it must undergo rigorous training and testing processes to ensure that its capabilities are enhanced and its limitations decreased.

Think about learning something at university. You go to different classes to master the profession that you want to carry out in the future. If you are a law student, you will have classes on different types of legislation, processes, and even courtroom behavior. However, as you train, you will become highly specialized in one matter or another. In the case of AI and LLMs, it is like learning the process for all areas in all places and building this cohesive knowledge to act as a legal aid anywhere in the world.

The learning process can be carried out through different approaches, either individually or together. Here is what you should know about each of them:

- **Supervised learning:** To understand supervised learning, consider a medical student learning from an experienced doctor. During the training, they will receive information that is validated, similar to what happens to AI systems. In this case, the program receives clear instructions and labeled examples. It will work in real life when you rate a movie on Netflix or mark an email in your inbox as spam. The system will receive direct feedback stating what it is supposed to do with that information. With millions of these interactions, the AI learns to recognize patterns and make better predictions. In healthcare, this might involve showing AI thousands of labeled medical images to help distinguish between different conditions.

- **Unsupervised learning:** When the unsupervised learning process is carried out, it is like opening a box of building blocks that you have to sort through color, size, and type without any previous information about what is in the box. When you shop online, for example, the AI might notice that people who often buy running shoes often purchase sports socks too, even though no one explicitly taught it this connection. To use a similar example in healthcare, it would be similar to analyzing millions of patient records to discover previously known relationships between symptoms, helping doctors identify new disease patterns.

- **Semisupervised learning:** To understand semisupervised learning, think about a medical resident who carries out procedures by themselves but has an attending to guide them through the process occasionally. This is the main foundation of this learning system, which can be found in modern voice assistants such as Siri or Alexa. In this case, they come pretrained on basic language, but learn your specific speech patterns and preferences through an initial voice recognition test and later through continued interaction; they start with a foundation but improve through regular use and feedback.

- **Reinforcement learning:** Think about reinforcement learning as the process that you would carry out with a pet. Similar to them, the AI system will learn through trial and error with clear rewards, such as earning a point in the system, or penalties, such as losing a point. In a practical example, consider ride-sharing apps optimizing routes: When drivers arrive quickly following a suggested route, the system receives positive feedback. If a route consistently causes delays, it learns to avoid it under similar conditions. In medical diagnosis, systems might receive positive feedback when their predictions match expert diagnoses and negative feedback when they miss important signs.

During the learning process, the AI system will constantly validate its knowledge by testing new examples they haven't seen before. When you provide feedback on product recommendations or adjust your home settings, you are helping these systems learn and improve. The entire process requires amazing computational resources and careful monitoring. This power is so amazing that modern AI systems can process more information in a day than a human would in several lifetimes.

Here, as you will explore further in the chapter, it is essential to be careful with the data you are presenting to the program. Just as we wouldn't want medical students to learn outdated treatments or develop biases, AI systems must be trained with diverse and accurate data that constantly undergo quality checks. This validation process is crucial to ensure the system truly learns rather than memorizes patterns.

What makes this different from learning is the scale and speed: While we might learn from hundreds of examples throughout the years, AI systems can process millions of examples in hours. This leads to an enhanced improvement in their capabilities in real time, as long as they receive quality feedback and data. Every time you interact with an AI system, you are contributing to this massive learning process.

This basic training process will then get refined and specialized for specific tasks, transforming broad knowledge into focused expertise. The next time you see a surprisingly accurate product recommendation, for example, or a voice assistant perfectly understanding your accent, remember that these are the result of the tiny lessons these machines are learning at a scale that would be impossible for any human to process. Yet, they must be carefully guided to avoid learning wrong lessons or developing biases, which is where pretraining and fine-tuning come in, as you are about to see next.

PRETRAINING AND FINE-TUNING

Developing an LLM is a two-step process that involves pretraining and fine-tuning. To understand these, picture a person who is just learning how to write. Pretraining would be leaving them in a library, which has different types of books including novels, encyclopedias, technical manuals, and even cookbooks. In this case, they will learn grammar, vocabulary, sentence structures, and even general knowledge.

Fine-tuning, on the other hand, is like giving this person a specific style guide and asking them to write a marketing piece, a blog post, or even a joke tailored to a specific audience. At the same time, this process is not as complex as it seems. When they are broken down into parts, as you will see next, the process becomes clearly understandable and brings insights into what these systems can do.

Pretraining

Pretraining is the foundation of all LLMs. This includes exposing the model to incredible amounts of data from books, websites, articles, and other places. The goal, in this case, is to help the model learn how language works. As the model and the algorithm understand each source it is given, they can see how words are formed, sentences are structured, and how meaning can change depending on the context.

If you have ever been to another country that speaks a language other than yours or have tried learning a new language, understanding this process is easier. Suppose you want to learn Spanish. You might start by listening to Spanish radio, reading Spanish newspapers, and watching TV shows in Spanish. Even if you don't understand a word right away, you can start picking up patterns and common words. Additionally, you will be able to recognize common phrases, sentence structure, and word use. Over time and with dedication, it is likely you will start to pick up a general understanding of the language and context.

For an LLM, the process is similar, but on a greater scale. The model processes billions of sentences and learns based on probability. This means it learns to understand what word is likely to come next, given the previous words. For example, if you type in, "The dog is eating a..." the machine is more likely to predict "bone" than "banana." When the machine applies probability based on what it has analyzed, it will generate more humanlike text based on how many times the same information was identified within the sources.

The difference between humans and machines, in this case, is that during the pretraining phase, the program does not know or understand facts or information the way we do. It simply becomes very good at predicting language patterns. In the case of the previous example, a human would know that dogs are more likely to eat bones than bananas, but the machine simply "knows" this because of the instances in which this same word formation appears. As a result, while it can generate coherent text about almost any topic, its responses may still be general or lacking in depth when asked about specific or ambiguous subjects.

Fine-Tuning

Once the pretraining is complete, the model can generate text for general purposes. However, most real-world applications require models to perform specialized tasks, such as answering customer queries, generating creative content, or summarizing legal documents. This is the part where the fine-tuning comes in.

This process involves taking the pretrained model and training it further on a narrower dataset tailored to a specific domain or task. For example, a company that develops virtual assistants for financial advisors might fine-tune a general LLM using data from financial reports, investment strategies, and client communications. This process helps the model be more accurate and reliable in that specific field. The same can be said about a company that decides to use LLMs for their chatbots. They will need to fine-tune the program to what their company does, specifications, and details that will enable them to help customers.

To relate this situation to real life, imagine a student who has completed a general degree in communications. They now want to become a sports commentator. To specialize, they start studying the rules of different sports, watching games, and practicing play-by-play commentary. While they already understand language and communication thanks to their degree, they now need this focused training to excel in the desired role. Fine-tuning works similarly: It helps an already well-trained model become an expert in a certain topic.

It is also important to know that fine-tuning can be done for tasks requiring specific writing styles. If a social media company wants a chatbot that writes playful and informative replies, it can fine-tune an LLM on a dataset containing lighthearted conversations, memes, and casual language. On the other hand, a law firm might fine-tune its model on formal legal texts to ensure it generates professional and precise responses.

Putting It All Together

Both processes you have read about—pretraining and fine-tuning—are essential for creating versatile and effective LLMs. While the pretraining phase will provide a broader knowledge base, fine-tuning can be used to ensure it can be applied in certain contexts. Without the first, the model wouldn't have a general understanding of language, and without the latter, it would struggle to accurately perform specialized tasks.

At the same time, while these are powerful techniques, they come with their own set of challenges. Pretraining usually requires enormous computational resources and vast datasets, which can be costly and time-consuming. Additionally, the data in pretraining can often lead to biases present in real-world text, leading to the same result in its outputs. Similarly, fine-tuning presents the risk of *overfitting*, especially if the dataset being used to do it is too small or too narrow, leading it to become overly specialized and lose its generalization abilities. Moreover, fine-tuning requires careful curation of the dataset to avoid introducing errors.

In both cases, these processes must not be carried out by automation. Human oversight is critical at every step, from selecting the data to evaluating the model's performance or ensuring ethical use. As you will explore in Chapter 9, the responsible use of LLMs requires continuous monitoring to mitigate these risks, which can even be harmful outputs.

However, before you can understand these challenges and obstacles and why they appear, it is crucial to understand the specific components that make up an LLM. While you have already read about tokens in the previous chapter, the following section will bring you a recap on the subject and include parameters and datasets. Understanding these will provide you with a clearer view of how these systems operate and why their outputs are produced in a specific way.

TOKENS, PARAMETERS, AND DATASETS

Many people often wonder what makes models such as ChatGPT, Llama, Gemini, or Microsoft Copilot so powerful. To give you this answer, we must break down their main components into three parts: parameters, datasets, and tokens. These elements are essential for any LLM, and each directly influences how well the model performs. They are similar to the bricks in the house or the ingredients in a recipe: each plays a critical role and the final result will depend on how they are combined. To better understand the role each of them has in these programs, this is exactly what we will do: examine each individually to understand their part in the final outcome.

Tokens

As you have seen in the previous chapter, *tokenization* is the process of breaking down words or phrases into tokens, a piece of text that can be a word, part of a word, or a character. In practice, LLMs don't always split sentences into full words, they use tokenization to make them easier to process. Think of tokens as individual notes in a piece of music. Just as a musician reads each note and plays it in sequence to create a melody, an LLM processes each token to generate coherent sentences. In this case, the more efficiently it can handle tokes, the better it can understand and produce language.

Parameters

Now, let's talk about parameters. They are like the adjustable dials inside the model that help it decide. When an LLM is pretrained, it learns patterns from its training data, and these are stored as parameters. Generally speaking, they determine how the model connects one token to the next and how it predicts what word should follow based on the context. In LLMs, parameters serve as the tool it can use to recall and apply its acquired knowledge.

The more parameters a model has, the better it becomes at capturing subtle language patterns and generating accurate responses. GPT-3, to name a popular example, has *175 billion* parameters. That is an incredible number, and it's one of the reasons why it can generate such humanlike text. At the same time, models with fewer parameters may struggle with complex language tasks because they do not have the same "memory" depth or robust pattern recognition systems.

Datasets

Finally, we have the third component: datasets. A dataset is the collection of text that the LLM will be trained on. During the pretraining phase, it will be exposed to massive datasets containing all types of text you can imagine, most of which are available online. You will learn where they come from in the next section. In the meantime, you should know that the size and quality of this dataset are extremely important since the model can only learn from what it has been shown. A diverse and comprehensive dataset allows the LLM to handle a large range of language tasks.

A special emphasis must be given to the dataset quality. A large but poorly curated dataset can introduce biases or errors into the model, just as bad ingredients can ruin a dish. That is why human oversight is so important during pretraining and fine-tuning, ensuring that the data the model is being exposed to is balanced and relevant.

How These Elements Word Together

As you might imagine, these three elements must work together seamlessly to ensure that the model presents its best performance. During the pretraining phase, the model will be given an enormous dataset and learn to predict the next token based on the tokens it has already seen. This process adjusts the model's parameters millions of times, gradually improving its ability to understand and generate language.

In the fine-tuning phase, the process will become more focused. The LLM will be trained on a narrower dataset specific to a particular task or industry. Suppose a company wants to create a virtual assistant for a travel agency. They might fine-tune the LLM using a dataset filled with travel guides, booking information, and customer queries. This way, the model becomes highly skilled at answering travel-related questions.

For an even simpler breakdown, look at the following example:

- **Tokens:** The model processes customer questions like *Can you recommend a hotel in Paris?* by breaking them down into tokens.
- **Parameters:** It uses billions of parameters to understand the context of the question and generate an appropriate response.
- **Datasets:** Thanks to its fine-tuning on the corresponding data, the model knows that *hotel* refers to accommodation and *Paris* to the city in France, not a person with the same name.

While having numerous parameters and a vast dataset can enhance an LLM's capabilities, more isn't always necessarily better. Overloading a model with parameters can make it slower and more resource-intensive, while a dataset that is too large might introduce noise or irrelevant information. Striking the right balance is key, and that is why fine-tuning a carefully selected dataset is often necessary to tailor the model for specific applications.

As you can imagine, the data given to these models is what determines its performance. Without vast and diverse datasets, even the most sophisticated models would struggle to produce meaningful results. The questions that remain, then, are: *Where does all this data come from? How do developers gather all this text? Are there any challenges in the process?* Read on to discover the answer to these and much more, giving you a full understanding of how these datasets can build effective models and bring to the surface unique challenges regarding ownership, privacy, and ethics.

WHERE DOES THE DATA COME FROM?

You already know that training an LLM requires exposing it to enormous amounts of text data. *But where does all this data originate?* Generally speaking, data for the training process to take place is sourced from publicly available text, licensed content, and in some cases, proprietary datasets. While this abundance of data is what makes these models powerful, it also created significant ethical and legal concerns, especially regarding data ownership, privacy, and bias.

Publicly Available Data

A significant portion of the data used to train LLMs comes from publicly accessible sources such as websites, blogs, forums, and social media platforms. Models like GPT and Llama have been trained on vast datasets scraped from the internet, which might include everything from Wikipedia articles to online reviews and technical documentation. The advantage of using this type of data is that it provides a broad and diverse set of language samples, covering everything from formal writing to casual conversation.

However, relying on internet data comes with its own challenges. First, not all publicly available content is high quality. Some data may be poorly written, factually incorrect, or even harmful, such as hate speech or misleading information. Since LLMs learn from everything they are exposed to, poor-quality data can degrade the model's performance or introduce harmful biases. Additionally, there are also legal concerns surrounding whether web-scraped data can be used without explicit permission from content creators.

Licensed and Proprietary Data

To overcome the limitations of public data, companies often incorporate licensed or proprietary datasets into the training process. Licensed data refers to content that is legally obtained through agreements with publishers, academic institutions, or other organizations. For example, a company might license a collection of scientific journals or business reports to improve its model's understanding of specialized fields.

Proprietary data, on the other hand, is information collected directly by the organization developing the model. This could include internal documents, customer support transcripts, or other business-specific content. Using proprietary data allows companies to fine-tune models for industry-specific tasks, such as legal research or financial analysis. While this type of data offers significant advantages, it also raises ethical questions such as who owns the data and how it should be handled.

Data Collection Challenges

Despite the power that comes from having access to vast datasets, collecting and using data for LLMs is not without its challenges. Some of these include

- **Data privacy and ownership:** One of the most common and urgent issues in LLM training is ensuring that the data used respects privacy laws and intellectual property rights. Many jurisdictions, such as the European Union (such as the GDPR), have strict regulations around privacy.; The US has HIPAA. If a dataset includes personal information without consent, it can lead to legal and ethical repercussions. Additionally, using copyrighted material without permission raises concerns about intellectual property rights.
- **Bias:** Since LLMs learn from the data they are given, any bias present in the data can be absorbed by the model. If a dataset predominantly consists of English language content from certain regions, the model may become biased toward those linguistic or cultural norms. This can result in incorrect responses or a limited understanding of diverse perspectives.
- **Quality vs. quantity:** As mentioned earlier, while having large datasets is important, the quality of what it will add to the LLM matters just as much. Poor-quality data can lead to models that produce unreliable or nonsensical responses. Balancing a dataset's size and quality is a constant challenge developers have to deal with when developing effective LLMs.

- **Ethical data use:** Lastly, there is an ongoing debate about the ethical implications of training LLMs on content created by individuals who do not give consent for their work to be used in this way. While scraping public data can provide valuable resources, it can also be seen as exploiting the intellectual labor of countless writers, artists, and content creators.

Despite these challenges, and you will learn about more throughout the book, the datasets used to train LLMs have undoubtedly unlocked new possibilities in AI. These models started a revolution in how we interact with technology, making it easier to create content, solve problems, and automate complex tasks. However, as powerful as they are, the ethical and legal concerns surrounding data use cannot be ignored.

CHALLENGES: BIAS, HALLUCINATION, ETHICAL CONCERNS, AND OTHERS

Although LLMs are incredible programs with diverse purposes, this does not mean that they come without challenges. They still have several imperfections and limitations that, if the user is unknowledgeable, may lead to mistakes. Most of these challenges come from how they are developed and trained, which makes it essential to have some guidance on their ethical, responsible, and effective use. Here are, nine of the most common limitations for LLMs where human insight is crucial:

- **Bias:** Since LLMs are trained on datasets reflecting the content available on the internet and other sources, biases in these places can be conveyed during the learning process. This bias can manifest in different ways, including stereotypes based on gender, race, or socioeconomic status. Reducing bias requires a careful review of the information being used and carrying out periodic audits.

- **Hallucinations:** When an LLM produces information that seems plausible but is entirely fabricated, this is known as an AI hallucination. This happens because the words are predicated on patterns rather than knowledge or understanding, leading it to "invent" facts and statements when responding to a prompt. These can be particularly problematic in areas that require accuracy and reliability, once again pointing to the need for human oversight during use.

- **Outdated information:** Most LLMs have a cutoff date, which is the date up to when the data was collected. This means that, unless they have access to web searches, these models will have a limited vision of current events, cultural trends, and breakthroughs. For example, if the program has a cutoff date of August 2024, it will now know who the president of the US is if there is an election held afterward.

- **Lack of contextual understanding:** It may seem that the LLM you are working with has convincing knowledge, but do not be fooled by this impression! These models do not have any consciousness or genuine comprehension, meaning they fail to grasp emotional context, sarcasm, or even complex queries. As a result, it can lead to irrelevant or misleading responses, especially when considering a user looking for advice. When using LLMs for critical issues, do not forget to use a human consultant to help you with the matter.

- **Difficulty with specialized jargon:** Most of the LLM tools in existence today on the market can handle general tasks with efficiency. However, they might struggle with domain-specific knowledge, especially if they were not fine-tuned for this purpose. This means struggling in fields such as medicine, law, or even engineering, leading to potential hallucinations and misinformation.

- **Inconsistent performance across languages:** English is usually the primary language in which LLMs are trained, meaning their performance in other languages can vary. Even though many of these models are multilingual, they often demonstrate reduced fluency and accuracy in languages with fewer digital resources or that are not as common.

- **Resource-intensive development and operation:** Training LLMs requires incredible computational resources, including significant energy use. This raises environmental concerns, as the carbon footprint of generating this processing power and its subsequent. Additionally, the high costs associated with training and developing these LLMs can create a technological gap between larger and smaller companies, especially for those looking for innovative systems.

- **Sensitivity to prompt phrasing:** LLMs are very sensitive to how you write prompts. Even the smallest change in wording or typing mistakes can generate different responses, frustrating users who are looking for consistent results. This makes it essential to have some knowledge of prompt engineering, which you will learn more about in Chapter 5.

- **Limited ability to verify sources:** The lack of ability to verify output accuracy is one significant challenge faced by LLMs. While today several tools are using citing options and resources to show where the data came from, it is still very much needed to cross-reference the information in the output with other sources and explore other possibilities. Even with the citing features, there are still imperfections, so it is always best to be safe and double-check the information before using it.

Understanding and addressing these challenges is essential so that we can start building trust in AI systems. While LLMs have already made significant contributions to the fields you have seen, their limitations remind us they are tools, not replacements, for human judgment. Addressing issues like the ones you have seen in this section ensures the technology is developed and used responsibly.

Now that you have this comprehensive view of AI, LLMs, and how they work, it is time to move on and explore some of the most popular LLMs available in the market today. In the next chapter, you will explore and learn more about tools such as ChatGPT, Claude, Gemini, and Llama. As you read, you will start to identify the best tools to help you with tasks while gaining insight into how different LLMs can be applied to solve daily problems.

EXPLORING THE MOST POPULAR LLMS

With so many options on the market, choosing the best LLM to work with can seem overwhelming. Millions of people use these tools daily, making it one of the fastest-growing industries in the present. Despite its millions of users, this rapid implementation is not just about numbers, it is a significant change in how we work. By the end of 2025, it is estimated that 50% of digital work is expected to be automated by companies using LLMs (Uspenskyi, 2024).

But how do I choose the best tool for me with so many options available? The first thing you should know is that it is a concentrated market: "In 2023, the world's top five LLM developers acquired around 88.22% of the market revenue" (Uspenskyi, 2024). As soon as OpenAI announced and released GPT-3, Big Tech rushed to start creating their own models. These include Google, Microsoft, Apple, and Meta, to name a few. Today, companies large and small are investing in creating and improving the technology, building models of their own, and increasing the supply of what we find in the market.

To help you understand how to make the best choice and find the most suitable one for your tasks, in this chapter, you will learn about six of the most popular platforms. These are general-purpose LLMs, each with its strengths and challenges and best applications. As you read, you will find that there is much more to the world of LLMs than GPT, and some may even surprise you! Read on if you are ready to learn more about these chatbots and see how they can be integrated into your daily life to make it a little easier.

CHATGPT

Do you remember the first time you heard about ChatGPT? Maybe it was at work, with a colleague showing you the incredible new release on the market or perhaps it was a friend who always stays ahead of tech trends. When the chatbot was released in November 2022, what started as mere intrigue for many quickly became a gold rush, forever changing how we deal with technology. Just a few days after its launch, it reached 1 million users, a number that reached an amazing 100 million by February 2023.

From there, the tool gained significant traction and continues to grow. Its versatility is usually considered one of its top advantages, since it can be used for brainstorming ideas, debugging code, and even asking questions on complex subjects. In its latest version, it can even look at images and engage in voice conversations, making it more like a digital assistant rather than a computer program.

ChatGPT is available in the free (and limited) and paid versions. In the free version, you can use prompts to conversate and use most of its features. However, it has a limit of queries you can carry out per period, there are speed limitations, and even some features are unavailable. On the other hand, you can also subscribe to the paid version, known as ChatGPT Plus, which costs $20 per month and brings an amazing toolkit to the table (*ChatGPT*, 2024). The paid tool thinks faster, has no limits, and includes Dall·E 3 to create images and analyze graphs.

The tool's greatest ability is to create relatable and everyday text, regardless of the audience to whom the information is directed. It can instantly adapt the language being used to the user's needs. It has also become the go-to tool for most users, meaning it gets trained and fine-tuned more often with use. Developers are using it to cut their time dedicated to coding, customer service teams are using it to respond to queries, and marketing teams leverage it for content creation.

Finally, the introduction of custom GPTs in the newest version to replace the plugins has been a game-changer. Companies are using the feature to create their own specialized version of GPT tailored to their needs, language, and style guide. Others, who are not as keen on doing so, simply use the standard GPTs available to all users to get answers on specific themes, obtain "expert" advice, and get a more fine-tuned response from the model.

At the same time, ChatGPT also has significant limitations. Although the tool currently can search the internet, it was trained only up to April 2024 and, unless you prompt the tool to use the search feature, it will automatically default to the training data. Another challenge is the high level of hallucinations the tool produces. In many cases, for the unadvised user, it can create misinformation by confidently speaking about elements it is unsure or incorrect about. Although the tool is usually right, it is essential to always double- and cross-check the information it produces.

The future is bright for ChatGPT, especially since with every update it becomes more capable, understanding, and helpful. Additionally, with paid features being constantly implemented into the free version, you can have a small taste of what to expect with the paid and more capable version. Still, it is essential to remember that no matter how perfect and humanlike the tool is, it is not meant to replace human expertise but rather assist and make our lives easier.

GEMINI

When ChatGPT was launched, Google was one of the first companies to start looking at how it could develop its own model. Initially, it launched Bard, which was often seen as a bad copy of ChatGPT with fewer features and more errors and hallucinations. However, in December 2023, the company rebranded and launched a new version now called Gemini. This change marked an important change in the company's strategy and AI capabilities.

One of the main differences of this chatbot is that it was built to be different from other tools, more specifically due to the fact it is multimodal, meaning it naturally understands and works with text, images, audio, video, and code. Differently from ChatGPT, which has Dall·E implemented as a separate feature (and what happens with many other tools), Gemini has all the features integrated as a whole. This means you can have a conversation with the program about a picture you just took, and the AI will understand what is in the image and relate it to information it finds across the web.

This, in fact, is yet another feature the program offers (and was one of the first to do so without cost), which is the integration with the internet and web searches. But what really sets the tool apart is its integration with Google's applications. These include Google Search, the Google Docs suite, and even Android. By using Gemini, you can use AI in the Google ecosystem, including extending to Gmail, Google Maps, and all the other tools the company offers.

The chatbot comes in three different versions, tailored to the user's needs. There is Gemini Ultra, the most advanced tool, which costs $19.99 per month. Then there is Gemini Pro, the tool that powers the free version, which is already incredible in itself. Finally, there is Gemini Nano, which is specifically designed to run directly on mobile devices. As you can see, there is a version of Gemini for everyone!

Its ability to connect to your Google account also allows Gemini to provide personalized assistance while maintaining privacy and security. This means you can go through your documents, photos, and every file stored in the cloud, and it will be able to answer questions without needing to look for more information. Features such as these prove to be useful when you are looking for an email you don't immediately recall or pictures you do not remember to have taken and need to find. This personal touch makes it feel less like a generic AI and more like an assistant that knows you and your workflow.

However, Gemini does not come without its own set of limitations. While integrating with Google apps is certainly an incredible feature, it can also feel limited if you do not use the company's products. Like other AI chatbots, it faces challenges such as hallucinations and requires fact double-checking, especially for critical information. Additionally, its multimodal capabilities, while impressive, still have a long way to go as it is not unusual to have it misinterpret complex visual or audio inputs.

On the other hand, for those already comfortable with using Google's ecosystem, Gemini is not just another tool, but an extension of the workplace. Looking ahead, the company's massive data advantage and integration with widely adopted tools means that the technology can evolve quickly and with precision. Today, the company works toward developing responsible AI with fewer biases and hallucinations, with promising results in studies published so far (*Gemini*, n.d.).

LLAMA

This chatbot is Meta's response to GPT, even if it wasn't the company's first priority back in 2022. At that time, Mark Zuckerberg was looking to invest in the metaverse and even changed the company's group name from Facebook, Inc. to Meta Platforms, Inc. due to its increasing investment in the technology (Thomas, 2021). However, when ChatGPT was launched, it led to one of the fastest changes in strategy the technology world has seen, as the company shifted billions in resources from virtual reality to AI. From this originated Llama (short for Large Language Model Meta AI).

One of the main distinguishing characteristics of the program is the philosophy that was used to build it: The model was released to the research community in early 2023 and by the middle of the same year, it had been launched as a full-scale open-source model. While companies such as Google and OpenAI kept the inner workings and code behind their powerful programs locked in secrecy, Meta went the other way and decided to give away the blueprint for one of the most sophisticated AI engines ever built.

The program's latest version, released in February 2024 and known as Llama 3, is available in three parameter sizes: 8B, 70B, and 400B (*Llama*, 2024). In its most powerful version, 400B, the tool showcases improvements in reasoning, mathematical concepts, coding, and word knowledge, leading to a significant improvement from the previous version. This, and the company's impressive reach with Instagram, Facebook, and WhatsApp has the market wondering what will come next.

What makes Llama 3 particularly interesting is the type of architecture that was used during development. According to the company, the new structure has led to a decrease in hallucinations, more nuanced responses, and better contextual understanding (*Introducing Meta Llama 3*, 2024). Some innovations in the model include a greater number of tokens used and a variety of learning and training strategies, allowing the model to specialize in different tasks. These new capabilities would be similar to having multiple experts on one problem and, instead of reading the full studies to understand the issue, they can do it at once.

At the same time, the company claims that the new Llama 3 model is not just about performance and increasing its capability. Meta has focused on making the model more efficient, requiring less computational power to run effectively, thus addressing critical elements such as energy use and the ability for other companies to implement the program. A smaller processing power means smaller organizations and researchers can work with the tool without needing massive computing resources, which essentially means making the technology available to all.

Nonetheless, even with its decreased computational power processing requirements, this does not mean that it is a cheap technology. To have the program work with the minimum parameters, hardware that is worth thousands of dollars is still needed. Additionally, without a controlled environment that systems like Gemini and GPT have, there is a greater risk of misuse or creation of harmful applications. To address the issue, Meta has included within its user and license agreements terms that include safety and ethical use requirements.

Finally, whether the company's decision to release Llama as an open-sourced software was a good decision still remains to be seen. On one hand, it allows the company to separate itself from competitors by empowering users and researchers to innovate and help them improve the model. On the other, it opens up the opportunity for ill-intentioned individuals and companies to take advantage of a superior technology for unlawful purposes. Whether this strategy will pay off is still unknown, but one thing is for sure: Meta changed the way we think about AI development and accessibility.

CLAUDE

When Anthropic, the creator of Claude, appeared with a new chatbot proposal to the market, the chatbot came with significant knowledge. The main reason for this is that it was founded by former OpenAI researchers who wanted to create more transparent and ethically aligned AI systems. To achieve this goal, the company took an approach of promoting honesty, allowing the tool to even admit when it doesn't know something.

One of the most interesting aspects of Claude is the fact that developers are not looking at what *to do* or features to add. Quite the contrary. They are exploring the elements and features that AI programs should or should not have. As it develops a system that is not shy of admitting it does not know or does not have the information, it brings a paradox and a different landscape to the AI industry. This approach comes from Anthropic's constitutional principles, which aim to create AI systems that are powerful, truthful, and aligned with human values (*Meet Claude*, 2024).

The tool's latest model, Claude 3.5, comes in three versions: Haiku, Sonnet, and Opus, each for different cases. Opus is the most capable version, with highly skilled reasoning, analysis, and problem-solving capabilities. At the same time, the tool also has free (Sonnet 3.5) and paid versions, (Haiku 3.5 and Opus 3.5); the latter costing $18 per month without VAT. What sets these models apart is their consistent approach to safety and transparency, allowing you to consider and reflect upon the implications of what the prompt is requesting.

While this might seem like the ideal tool, being so ethically inclined comes with its own challenges. The tool's constraints sometimes mean that it will fail to help you when other tools might. This excess of caution reflects on the chatbot's speed since answers can be considerably slower when compared to its competitors. Therefore, most of its applications are for where certainty is essential, such as in healthcare and legal industries, education, and research and analysis.

Conversely, one of its most distinctive features is its approach to cutoff dates, an element that other chatbots fail to acknowledge. Rather than pretending to know about recent events or making assumptions, the model clearly communicated its knowledge limitations and suggested verifying current information from reliable resources. This honesty is limiting, but it builds trust with users who need reliable information. Additionally, it can search the internet, but in the free version, this can consume a significant amount of tokens, leading to waiting times to have longer conversations.

Although Claude does not have the massive user base of ChatGPT, which allows the tool to be constantly trained or the integration and multimodal features of Gemini, it is a promising tool for those looking for reliable information. It has created a base of loyal users who prioritize reliability and ethics with their AI use. Its ability to handle complex documents, engage in discussions, and maintain consistent behavior made the tool indispensable in regulated industries and educational and research institutions.

MICROSOFT COPILOT

If you are a user of Microsoft 365, you have probably noticed that new updates have quietly been added to its applications. Microsoft Copilot, previously known as Bing Chat, is one of the most audacious integrations of AI into everyday tools. If you imagine the number of people using Microsoft programs and the impact that using and implementing AI into them can have, you will understand why the tool is considered a game-changer in the market. In addition to this, Microsoft combines its AI capabilities with an impressive cloud environment in Azure and its several years of experience in the technology market.

To name a few examples:

- In Word, documents can be drafted, edited, and summarized.
- In Excel, data and formulas can be analyzed.
- In PowerPoint, presentations can be generated with a simple prompt.
- In Outlook, draft emails can be written in specific tones, and email threads can be summarized.
- In Teams, meeting summaries and action items can be automatically generated.

However, the tool's most important feature is the ability to understand context. Suppose you are working on a document, the chatbot will see the text and understand its purpose, analyze your previous work patterns, and the idea behind what you are creating. When this happens, the tool can offer suggestions that are more relevant to the content you are creating, rather than giving you a generic response that other AI models would.

Since the Microsoft suite is mostly dedicated to corporate and enterprise users, the company built the model considering special circumstances for privacy and security. To ensure this happens, Copilot operates within Azure, Microsoft's secure cloud infrastructure, ensuring the entered data does not leave the business's environment. This means they can enhance the application of the company's data protection protocols and prevent the information from leaving the corporate environment.

Although it has impressive capabilities within the Microsoft suite, its capacity extends beyond this primary use. Microsoft Copilot is also able to develop code, write cohesive text, and troubleshoot Windows problems. Its access to the internet enhances search and browsing experiences with AI-powered insights. The company's idea is to bring an all-in-one solution that will increase its use within other organizations.

This integration, at the same time, comes at a cost, especially for those looking to scale their operations and deploy the system throughout businesses. The subscription model is particularly expensive for these, with proposals being tailored to each need. Similarly, the experience of having AI embedded in all programs you are using might seem overwhelming—and even excessive—to some users. It is also important to mention that there is a learning curve in understanding how to effectively prompt Copilot for optimal results.

Microsoft's AI implementation across its multiple programs stands as an example of what the future might look like. In it, rather than being presented as a standalone solution, LLMs and AI chatbots are set to become virtual assistants embedded in most of the programs we use. While on one side it will enhance user experience and allow for a more productive workspace, it is essential to think about what it would mean for one company to manage all this information, especially with the increase in cyber threats.

GROK

In November 2023, Elon Musk revealed Grok to the world, an LLM created by his company xAI that had a mission different from other AI virtual assistants. It was designed to have a sarcastic, irreverent, and witty personality, setting the tone of how it would be used. The tool was first developed to be used with X (formerly Twitter) and is still limited to a "Fun Mode" (Research Graph, 2024).

xAI's idea was to develop a tool that maximizes curiosity and seeks truth, making it even more interesting as it has real-time access to X's database. Its approach is to be direct and even *engage* in controversial topics on social media, many including subjects other platforms would avoid. While it has a certain liberty to engage, provoke, and answer to these, xAI ensures it has built-in measures to prevent harmful comments.

This approach to AI development has led Grok to have a few, but loyal users. It is still a limited tool, restricted only to X's Premium subscribers for $16 a month, and there is no report of expanding the tool. It serves the purpose for which it was created: engaging an especially dedicated audience who are looking for more personality-driven and entertainment-focused AI tools that are not afraid to challenge conventions (*xAI: Understand the Universe*, 2025).

Grok is still quite different from other LLMs, but it shows an illustration of what could happen in the future. With its transparency, truthful, and personality-filled features, not to mention data analysis in real-time, it can be a game-changer in the market. This means that we might be looking at AI systems chosen not only by their capabilities but also by their communication style.

While xAI has not yet released any information to date on future implementations, increasing Grok's capabilities is within its plans. With the range of Musk's empires, it would be no surprise to soon see the LLM in other tools developed by the mogul's companies, leaving open the question of its impact on the AI industry. For some, this might be a new way to communicate on social media and for tasks that do not require professionalism or educational features. For others, it is a tool that might never be used, especially considering current adoption rates and limitations to X.

The key here is to see if this approach to AI assistants is sustainable in the future. Today, many people look for tools that can help them carry out multiple tasks, and if a tool is seen as limited, it might not reach the expected numbers. It certainly adds questions and flavors to what some consider "boring" and "mechanical" writing, but how far it will go remains a question.

As you continue to read, it is important to keep in mind that no AI tool is perfect and that many of them have different but significant limitations. Each is ideal for a set of tasks, representing a vision of how AI can increase our productivity and enhance our lives and work. But having access to these tools is just the beginning.

Now that you have understood how AI and LLMs learn and operate and the main competitors in the market, it is finally time to learn how to interact with them. You might wonder why some responses are different from others, and why some people have more success using these LLMs than others. The answer is actually simple: They have started to master the art of *prompt engineering.*

In the next chapter, you will learn the secrets of how to effectively communicate with these programs, learning to prompt the machine to give you exactly what you need. Just as you would learn any other language, in this case, you will be learning "AI language," allowing you to achieve the best results during your interaction. If you are ready to start taking some notes and testing prompts, read on. There is still much to learn, see, and do!

UNDERSTANDING PROMPT ENGINEERING

Think about all the people you know. Certainly, one of them is the type who can always get what they want, especially because they can explain exactly what they want or need simply and concisely. Instead of asking "Can you help me with this document?" they will say, "I need help fact-checking this document. My deadline is in two hours." The first, as you might imagine, opens up several possibilities, while the second gives the individual exactly the person's needs and time to conclude it.

The same principle can be applied to AI programs and prompt engineering. How you speak to the machine will determine exactly what the output will be and if it will be useful or not. It is the difference between receiving a generic response and a more precise one. Today, prompt engineering is not just some new fancy word—it is the key that will give you access to using LLMs efficiently.

This chapter's objective is to give you the necessary tools to achieve this, obtaining insightful analysis that matches your needs. You will learn about the principles that make prompts effective and the structures that deliver results, see examples of how to put these into practice, and discover advanced techniques to enhance your experience. It does not matter for what purpose you are using the tool: By understanding prompt engineering, you will start to get better results immediately! Are you ready to see how?

Author's note: As you have seen in the last chapter, there are several LLMs to consider, and each has its unique approach to prompts. The structures you will see in this chapter can be applied to most of these tools, with some fine-tuning needed. Due to the number of users and market reach, the structures and information you will see in this chapter will be based on results produced by ChatGPT.

WHAT IS PROMPT ENGINEERING?

Prompt engineering is the action of writing effective inputs for AI language models to generate optimal results. It involves designing, refining, and optimizing text prompts that will allow you to achieve optimal outputs and meaningful responses. Being able to generate these inputs is so significant that a whole new career has been developed for it, and specialists in the subjects are known as *prompt engineers*. However, prompt engineering is not only for specialists. With some knowledge, you can also learn this skill and become a specialist at extracting useful answers from LLMs.

As mentioned earlier, learning about prompt engineering is much like learning a new language. Only, instead of speaking to another human, you will be doing so to a machine that thinks and responds similarly to how humans do. At the same time, while powerful, they process information differently, with patterns, as you have also seen before. Therefore, it is essential to learn how to structure our requests to help the models better understand what our intentions and needs are so responses are useful.

You might be thinking, *If this is something professionals do, it might require some intensive studying and learning.* The answer to this statement is both "yes" and "no." To address the first, yes, you will need to understand the different techniques and strategies that can be used, including the formatting choices and what exactly you are going to ask. This might include providing context, setting constraints, offering examples, or even breaking tasks into smaller parts. You must learn not only *what* to ask but also *how* to ask.

While this might initially seem overwhelming, you do not have to worry! Unlike other spoken languages, once you understand the main concepts, you will be able to seamlessly implement them, especially since most of the prompts follow a similar structure. There is also a secret: Mastering "AI language" is similar to speaking to a child or giving direct instructions to someone who gets frequently confused. As you will see, it is about getting the best possible response, not just *any* response.

Why It Matters

Just by the previous explanation, you might be starting to get the big picture of why prompt engineering is so important. Today, with more AI and LLM-fueled applications being presented to us at work, school, and home, knowing how to use prompt engineering is not just a nice-to-have, but essential. To summarize its importance: Poor prompt engineering can lead to subpar and even misleading results, while well-crafted prompts can help decrease the time to carry out a task from hours to minutes.

Suppose you are a history teacher in a class full of students. You are explaining to them the events that led up to and succeeded World War I when a student asks, "But I don't understand World War I." This question is too broad, and you catch yourself thinking, *What about World War I don't they understand?* The same concept applies to AI. When you are writing a prompt, you must tell it the desired tone, structure, format, and intended audience so it can provide you with an accurate response.

A few other reasons to learn prompt engineering include:

- Maximize efficiency and resource use, reducing the number of iterations needed to achieve outcomes.
- Prevent hallucinations and off-topic responses, ensuring more reliable and consistent results.
- Create a connection between human intention and machine capability, ensuring your needs are met instead of adapting to the tool's limitations.
- Stay up-to-date with the market, allowing you to implement AI use in your personal and professional lives.

When you learn how to ask, you will see that speaking to LLMs will become second nature to you. You will see that the outcomes you obtain are better and that you spend less time achieving goals with the program. You will become empowered to use AI's full potential and use these tools as partners that help you solve complex problems or automate tasks. *And how do I achieve this?* you might ask. Well, read on to find out!

EFFECTIVE PROMPTS: KEY PRINCIPLES

The essence of creating a prompt is to efficiently and clearly communicate your intent to the machine. When prompts are specific, well-structured, and easy to understand, LLMs are more likely to provide accurate and relevant results. To help you master the skill, you will now see a list of *dos* and *don'ts* to start practicing and have a greater understanding of what AI prompts should look like.

Dos

- **Be specific:** The more clear your prompts are, the more focused the answers will be. When the task is objective and detailed, the model can avoid producing broad or irrelevant information:

- *Instead of:* "Explain marketing."
- *Use:* "Explain three principles of digital marketing for small businesses."

- **Use simple language:** Although most LLMs are trained in different types of languages, avoid using complex or technical language unless necessary. This helps avoid confusion and improves output accuracy.
  - *Instead of:* "Articulate the economic ramifications of fiscal policy alterations."
  - *Use:* "Explain how changes in the government affect the economy."

- **Break down complex requests:** If what you need requires several steps, the best idea is to break them down into parts to improve coherence and avoid hallucinations. This always makes fact-checking easier and faster.
  - *Instead of:* "Write a report on climate change and renewable energy."
  - *Use:* "Write a brief summary on climate change. Then list five types of renewable energy with a short explanation for each."

- **Provide context:** Providing the LLM with background information helps the tool better understand what you need. Without context, the response may be too generic or off-topic.
  - *Instead of:* "How does blockchain work?"
  - *Use:* "How does a blockchain system verify transactions?"

- **Determine the audience:** Since the LLM can adapt the language and tone of the message, it is essential to tell it who the intended audience is. This allows you to adjust the content to different people and increase comprehension.
  - *Instead of:* "Explain the seasons."
  - *Use:* "Explain the seasons as you would to a seven-year-old."

- **Use examples:** Including an example of the output you wish to receive allows the model to understand what you are looking for. This is especially useful for formatting and tone adjustments.

- *Instead of:* "Write an email to a client answering a complaint."
- *Use:* "Write a polite email to a client to apologetically answer a complaint."

- **Ask for explanations:** Requesting detailed explanations and step-by-step responses helps the machine to understand better what you need and also allows you to have a better comprehension of the output.

  - *Instead of:* "Explain why it rains."
  - *Use:* "Explain why it rains step-by-step with a brief description of each process."

- **Ask for sources:** Since there is a possibility that the AI tool might hallucinate, depending on the topic you are researching, you should include the request for sources. This will speed up fact-checking time and allow you to establish credibility.

  - *Instead of:* "Give me a list of things I must take when considering camping during the winter."
  - *Use:* "Give me a list of things I must take when considering camping during the winter. Provide sources."

- **Test and refine:** Effective prompting will usually involve trial and error until you find the correct flow. If the first response you receive is not what you were expecting, refine the prompt to get better results.

  - *Use:* "Include detailed examples," "Can you explain it in simpler terms?" "Provide more information," or, "Be more specific."

- **Provide feedback:** Although the tool will learn based on your interactions, if you do not provide feedback on the output it is providing you with, it will never identify where it is getting it wrong. Use thumbs-up, stars, or other feedback mechanisms available in these chats to let it know your level of satisfaction with the tool.

Don'ts

- **Be vague:** Vague prompts lead to board or irrelevant responses. When you provide clear instructions, it ensures that the AI understands exactly what you want.
  - *Instead of:* "Tell me something about history."
  - *Use:* "Summarize the causes of World War II."
- **Use ambiguity:** Ambiguous words can confuse the AI, resulting in inaccurate responses. Where possible, use words that have a clear meaning and ensure that the context does not allow for double interpretation.
  - *Instead of:* "Explain the principle."
  - *Use:* "Explain the principle of supply and demand in economics."
- **Input too much information:** Giving the LLM too many instructions might confuse it, especially if the tasks are not related. This can lead to disorganized or incomplete answers.
  - *Instead of:* "Describe the impact of the Industrial Revolution on society, technology, and politics."
  - *Use:* One prompt for each piece of information you want to talk about.
- **Use excessive jargon:** Specialized terms without explanation can confuse general-purpose models. Use simple terms and provide definitions and context when necessary to make the instructions clearer.
  - *Instead of:* "Describe the process of cytokinesis in the miotic division."
  - *Use:* "Using simple terms, describe the cell division process, particularly cytokinesis."
- **Assume the machine knows your intent:** Since AI programs do not understand feelings or comprehend what you are asking about, you must not assume that it knows the prompt's intent. If there is a specific answer or reason for what you are doing, explicitly state it so the model can understand.

- *Instead of:* "Talk about the advantages and disadvantages of renewable energy."
- *Use:* "I am preparing for a debate and would like to know five pros and five cons of renewable energy."

- **Ignore feedback:** If your request was not fulfilled, maybe you need to adjust or refine the prompt instead of repeating it verbatim. Learning from this feedback helps you refine results over time.
  - *Use:* Prompt adjustments and refinement, rephrasing the prompt, asking it a different way, review to see what information is missing.
- **Expect perfection:** While this might seem obvious, it is important to state that AI models are far from perfect. Yes, they can provide helpful information, but you should always review critical information to ensure accuracy, cohesion, and completeness.
  - *Use:* Human oversight and critical thinking to verify the provided output and check for sources if you are in doubt regarding the information.

By following these dos and don'ts, you will be able to start your experience with LLMs. As practice, I would suggest that you now put this book aside for a minute and open your preferred program. Try adding the prompts you have seen to the dialogue and explore the answers it will give you. You can start with generic questions and then create a more suitable alternative to the one you have just read. Take some time to practice and see the differences that using these simple rules will make.

Once you are done, come back so you can start to explore different prompt structures to use for multiple purposes. Not only will you see templates that can be easily adjusted, but you will also see detailed examples of how different prompts can bring you very distinct results. What are you waiting for? Grab a computer and try some of these out!

PROMPT STRUCTURES AND EXAMPLES

In the previous section, you have read about the dos and don'ts of prompts. But did you know that there are certain structures you can follow to achieve the best results? This means not just typing in a question or a line of text to obtain the relevant output. These are structured prompts, each with a specific purpose that can be more effective in certain circumstances instead of others. Here are the main types of prompt structures and how you can use them in daily situations.

Prompt type	Use	Structure	Example
Directive prompts	• specific and focused outputs with minimal deviation • limited time and focus on efficiency	• clear command or instruction • specific parameters or constraints • desired format or output styles	*Write a professional email template following up with clients who haven't responded in 30 days. Use a friendly but professional tone and include a placeholder for customer name and previous interaction details.*
Conversational prompts	• use a more natural and dialogue-based approach • engage the AI iteratively and collaboratively • obtain detailed responses	• natural language phrasing • set context • use open-ended questions or situations	*I am preparing for a major client presentation next week. Can you help me think about how to structure it? The client is a retail company looking to improve their online presence. I want to ensure pain points are covered while showcasing solutions.*

Context-rich prompts	• complex tasks that need a nuanced understanding • consider multiple factors • customization is important	• detailed background information • requirements or constraints • target audience • desired outcome or objective • relevant examples	*Our software company is launching a new project. Target audience: small to medium-sized businesses (10–50 employees). Current market pain points: complex interfaces, poor mobile integration, and pricing transparency. Create a marketing strategy that will address the audience and their pain points in different channels.*
Role-based prompts	• specialized expertise • specific perspective • industry-specific jargon	• clear role assignment • specific task or question • relevant context • level of expertise	*You are an experienced financial analyst who will review our company's investments. Review our company's investment portfolio and provide recommendations for rebalancing, considering market conditions and our goal of moderate growth and risk mitigation.*
Zero-shot prompts	• no examples to give the machine • to be used with highly capable models	• straightforward tasks • effective results • quick activities	*Generate five names for a new eco-friendly cleaning product brand.*

Template prompts	• to obtain consistent structures for repeated tasks • uses placeholders you can fill in • standardizing outputs • maintaining consistency	• elements needed must be in between square brackets • clear instructions stating what you need • title, structure, problem, requirements, context, and constraints	*I need to build customer files with standardized information and order. The information must be complete with [insert information needed] and the output should be [describe].*
Comparative prompts	• compare and contrast different information	• provide the elements you want to compare and the context in which the comparison will be used	*Compare these three marketing channels for my startup:* 1. *Social media advertising* 2. *Content marketing* 3. *Email campaigns*

These basic prompt structures will provide you with the necessary tools to start working with LLMs. At the same time, they will be useful tools to help you start with advanced prompting techniques, which can transform your interactions with AI from simple question-and-answer exchanges into incredible problem-solving partnerships. In the final section of this chapter, you will explore advanced techniques that separate casual users from those who can obtain the best results.

ADVANCED PROMPTING TECHNIQUES

If you are looking to use AI to leverage your business's capabilities or to start a side income activity, advanced prompting techniques can be the key to helping you unlock the best results. The techniques you will see in this last section will help you deal with complex challenges, generate creative content, and develop innovative solutions, even if this means starting a business from scratch. These are strategies that those with experience in AI commonly use to increase productivity and efficiency.

Iterative Refinement

One of the advantages of using LLMs is that you can carry out conversations with them, meaning that you can refine the result as it is given. In this case, you will need to undergo several rounds of prompting, asking questions, and guiding the machine until it reaches the desired output. This would be similar to making a sculpture, in which you would start with a rough shape and gradually refine it until you reach the desired result.

An example of iterative prompting would be

- *Initial prompt:* "Write a product description for an online translation service for ecommerce."
- *Refinement 1:* "Make the description more technical, including the areas in which it can help."
- *Refinement 2:* "Add to the description the number of languages that can be used."
- *Refinement 3:* "Include the options of machine-performed and human-performed translations and editing."

This technique will help you ensure that each iteration builds upon previous responses while adding new layers of detail and precision to the final output.

Chain-Of-Thought Prompts

Similar to the iterative prompting process, when you use the chain-of-thought prompts, you will ask the machine to carry out different activities by breaking the task into smaller steps. In this case, each output will be what feeds the next prompt, allowing you to maintain a chain of thought throughout the process. One example of these types of prompts is:

Prompt 1: Analyze these customer service responses and identify key themes.

[output]

Prompt 2: Using these themes, draft a potential solution approach.

[output]

Prompt 3: Based on these solutions, create an implementation timeline.

[output]

Prompt 4: Generate a presentation outline incorporating the analysis, solutions, and timeline.

While this structure is similar to what you have seen in the previous section on *conversational prompts*, it is different because you are breaking the steps as the outputs are being given. Additionally, you are *building* on them, which is a difference, especially in the results that will be generated.

Few-Shot Prompts

These prompts will allow you to first show the machine examples of the inputs you will give and the outputs you expect. After this has been done, you will be able to give it the main task, which should mimic the information you provided. This structure is especially effective for establishing patterns and ensuring consistent formatting. Here is an example:

Prompt 1:

Example 1:

Product: Wireless headphones.

Description: Premium noise-canceling headphones with a 30-hour battery life, perfect for professionals on the go.

Prompt 2:

Example 2:

Product: Smart water bottle.

Description: Tracks hydration levels and reminds you to drink water throughout the day.

Prompt 3: Now write a description for:

Product: Smart home security camera

By implementing this strategy, you can standardize product and service descriptions on webpages, ensuring your company adopts the same tone throughout the channel. These can also be used for social media posts, emails, and other business tasks that must be standardized or have a similar format.

Constraint-Based Prompts

In the real world, sometimes we need solutions but face constraints to make it happen just as we would like. In this case, you can use constraint-based prompts to help you find the best alternative among the options. To do this, you will need to tell the machine what the constraints are and what it is expected to do, as follows:

Prompt: "Generate a marketing campaign concept that uses not more than a $5,000 budget, must include social media and email, cannot use paid advertising, and must be measurable within 30 days."

By giving the machine the limitations you face for the task at hand, it will be able to obtain different points of view and opportunities to explore. At the same time, this does not mean that you need to be restricted to just one type of prompt. You can use these different structures and combine them to achieve the best outputs for your company. In this case, you could associate a role-based prompt with a constraint-based prompt to help you obtain more specific information, such as:

> *Prompt:* You are an experienced marketing specialist used to working with companies with limited budgets. Generate a marketing campaign concept that uses not more than a $5000 budget, must include social media and email, cannot use paid advertising, and must be measurable within 30 days.

You can combine any type of structures you have seen so far or even create new ones of your own. As you continue to gain practice in prompting and speaking with LLMs, especially depending on the AI you choose, you will be able to find the strategy that best works for you. Remember: You can use together any of these you have seen, as long as they are clear, direct, and understandable.

Meta Prompts

Did you know that you can have the chatbot create the prompt for you? While many people do not know this, it is certainly a possibility that can be explored, especially in those times when the AI does not seem to be understanding you. In this case, you will use meta prompts, which are used to generate or improve other prompts, helping you to optimize the interaction with the machine. This can be done as follows:

Prompt: "Help me create an effective prompt for generating product descriptions. The prompt should ensure consistent tone and style, and inclusion of key features and benefits, appropriate length and format, and compelling call-to-action."

Once you input this information or any other that you need into the machine, you will see the magic happen. While you might need to adjust and refine the prompt the machine gives you, it is already halfway on the path to achieving optimal results. It is also a great opportunity for you to practice and see the best types of prompts you can create, refining your new skill for what is next to come.

As you continue to practice and master prompt engineering, you will enhance how you interact with AI systems. You should remember that the ability to write effective prompts is not just about the answer you will get, but also about how you can connect to the machine so that it understands you. The skills you have learned in this chapter will be essential for the next parts of this book, in which you will learn how to leverage these machines to your advantage.

The first stop is how you can use AI to increase productivity and business, allowing you to discover how these tools can help you streamline workflows, enhance decision-making, and drive business value. You will understand how to make yourself more productive by using technology to carry out basic tasks and for professional success. It is now time to move on from theory to practice that will drive tangible and real-world results. Are you ready?

USING AI FOR PRODUCTIVITY AND BUSINESS

I t is undeniable that AI will continue to change the world in almost all aspects we can think of. As it reshapes how companies carry out their business, it is essential to understand how to effectively leverage AI tools regardless of the industry you are in. So far, we have covered the theoretical aspect of AI systems and LLMs, but now it is time to see how this can be put into practice, which is what this chapter is all about.

From tools that are built exclusively on top of LLM models to programs that can analyze data and create cohesive text, there is an AI for almost any task you want to carry out. You will see how these tools can be integrated into your workflow and automate routine tasks to be more productive. Additionally, you will learn how these models can enhance your decision-making processes using advanced user business analytics.

POPULAR TOOLS BUILT ON LLMS

Since ChatGPT was released, the number of AI models available to the public has significantly increased. These tools have transformed from simple automation aids into sophisticated assistants that can handle complex tasks and enhance productivity. From industry-specific applications to the more general models you have already seen, some of the popular tools you are about to read about might even surprise you!

- **Jasper:** Tools such as these have completely changed how marketing teams carry out their work. With it, you can create multiple campaigns across different channels, even if you are on a tight deadline. Another advantage of this LLM is that it can generate initial drafts and maintain a consistent voice as well as tone throughout different channels. The AI's ability to understand context and adapt tone according to theme and instructions has made the tool a must-have for content teams globally.

- **GitHub Copilot:** For software developers, GitHub Copilot has proven to be an invaluable asset, especially for programming tasks. With it, even junior developers can code as if they had an experienced professional helping them, offering suggestions, and helping address challenges. This has increased tech professionals' productivity and allowed them to even work with unfamiliar code. Its ability to troubleshoot based on the knowledge it was trained on allows millions of lines to be debugged and improved in seconds, speeding up the development process and improving code accuracy.

- **Notion AI:** This tool has become widely popular in business environments, especially due to its versatility. The AI assistant allows teams to collaborate and organize information, allowing daily workflows to be enhanced. Some of its features include the ability to draft documents, summarize meetings, and manage projects. While this is one of the most popular tools on the market, powered by ChatGPT and Claude, others are also gaining traction, due to their abilities to understand context and generate relevant content for teams that need to collaborate in person or remotely.

- **Grammarly:** One of the most popular tools on the market today is this AI-powered app that has become a must for those who work with written content. Especially in the Business version, the app goes beyond simple grammar checking and becomes a writing assistant to help maintain communication consistent and well-written. With its different features to adjust tone and other settings for text correction and adjustment, you can use it to proof and review text so that it is aligned with your brand voice and the highest professional standards.

- **Harvey AI:** Professionals in the legal industry are irreplaceable, but this does not mean there aren't AI tools that can help carry out some of their tasks. This LLM is one of the most used among these professionals, especially due to its wide range of abilities that include contract analysis to case law research. Although the information still must be fact-checked, and it is essential to use with human oversight, tools such as these allow the legal back office process to be faster and more streamlined, reducing costs associated with research and drafting times.

- **Elicit:** It would only be natural that if all other industries have tools that target their needs, the research community would have a few as well. In this case, Elicit is a platform that helps researchers fine-comb vast amounts of academic literature, synthesize findings, and identify relevant studies. This process is extremely efficient and has reduced the time needed for these processes, allowing researchers to focus more on analysis and interpretation.

Tools such as these continue to evolve at an amazing pace, with new features and capabilities being regularly added to increase their power. One of the most important aspects to consider is integration—by looking for tools that have APIs and native connections to popular business applications. This process leads to more robust workflows where AI assistance is available where and when needed.

These capabilities have also been seen in tools that we explored in previous chapters, such as Gemini for the Google suite and Microsoft Copilot for Microsoft applications. As organizations adopt these tools, they are finding out that the real power is not just in each application's capability, but in how they can be combined to create efficient workflows. A marketing team, for example, might use Jasper for content creation, Grammarly for refinement, and Notion AI for organization and collaboration. Associating these tools will allow the content production pipeline to be more comprehensive and free of errors.

At the same time, it is important that when selecting these tools, companies look at the immediate and future needs. It is important to consider tools that are scalable at a reasonable cost and that will support the company. The best tools offer scalability, allowing teams to expand their usage as comfort and capabilities grow. Other factors that should also be considered include data security and the level of customization available to meet specific industry or organizational requirements.

As powerful as these specialized tools are for enhancing productivity, the power of AI lies in its ability to analyze complex data and support strategic decision-making. Although content creation and task automation tools streamline operations, an AI's analytical capability can change how your company understands its data, identifies patterns, and makes informed decisions. Read on to learn more about these practical applications in business intelligence and decision-making processes, transforming data into actionable insights that lead to strategic change.

AI FOR ANALYSIS AND DECISION-MAKING

Decision-making is one of the most complex and challenging tasks of engaging in business. When action is needed, you must look into different aspects of the same situation, and it is not uncommon to miss data simply because the relationships are not seen. When you use

AI-powered tools, it is like gaining a super-powerful ally that will transform raw data into actionable insights. Using these systems can help uncover patterns and opportunities that might otherwise remain hidden, thus changing how business strategies and operations are carried out.

Think about your business and how you carry out your workflow. Now, take a moment to consider your market intelligence needs. Tools like Forrester AI and Crayon can serve as your digital market research team, working 24/7 to keep you informed. These systems enable you to track movements made by competitors and also alert you to emerging trends before they become obvious to the market. This means that you could spot a shift in consumer preferences or an emerging technology months before other companies, giving you the time to adapt your strategy and maintain your competitive edge.

Now, suppose that your needs are more financially related. There are AI tools for that too! By using apps such as Alphasense and Bloomberg AI, you can reduce the time spent on research while improving insight quality. These tools can, among other things, analyze earning calls, financial reports, and market indicators in real time, helping you make more informed investment decisions. Leveraging such tools allows you to have in one place a team of expert analysts tirelessly working to identify opportunities and risks in your financial health.

Another area that can also be significantly affected by AIs and LLMs is the supply chain. These operations can benefit from tools such as Blue Yonder and o9 solutions to manage and optimize your supply chain for the future. Implementing these into your workflow will allow the business to predict demand more accurately, optimize inventory, and receive warnings about potential disruptions. This means you can maintain optimal inventory levels while reducing costs and improving customer satisfaction, ensuring the products that are close to running out are always available.

Speaking about customers, businesses must understand their needs and demands to ensure profitable growth. Tools like Medallia and Qualtrics can analyze customer feedback across all business channels, helping you understand what customers are saying and feeling. As you leverage these tools, you will be able to predict customer behavior, identify at-risk accounts before they churn, and personalize your service approach based on nuanced insights.

Finally, when it comes to risk management, platforms such as RiskThinking.AI and Logic Manager can serve as early warning systems. They will help you identify potential risks across your operations, assess likelihood and potential impact, and suggest mitigation strategies. When you use AI for a proactive approach to risk management, you can avoid costly surprises and maintain business stability while having different variables analyzed to ensure you have the full picture.

As you can see, the prospects of AI tools for your company are vast and will depend on what you are looking for. To make the most of your selection, you must focus on three key areas:

1. Ensure your data is clean and well-integrated, especially since these systems are only as good as the data they work with.
2. Maintain appropriate human oversight. AI is valuable and can be very powerful, but your judgment and industry expertise remain crucial.
3. Invest in training for your team to ensure they can use these tools effectively and interpret their outputs.

As AI continues to evolve, it is more than likely these tools will continue to become even more powerful and sophisticated. Soon, they will be able to integrate data from more sources, provide clearer explanations for their recommendations, and adjust their analysis in real time, perhaps without even needing to upload data. This increase in capacity will lead to increased automation of routine decisions, thus allowing you to focus on more strategic parts of the business.

But how do I know the best tool to choose for me? The key to success is to carry out the necessary due diligence and understand their capabilities and features. Doing so will allow you to see which the right ones for your specific needs are and implement them thoughtfully. Start by identifying your most pressing analytical needs and the area your company needs the most insight. These can include market intelligence, financial analysis, risk assessment, customer insights, or any other area that you believe needs more information. Then, you should look for tools that will meet those needs and integrate well with your existing systems and processes.

While these tools will give you a significant advantage over other companies that do not have them, you must remember that it is your experience, judgment, and understanding of the business context that will turn the insights you derive from these tools into effective decisions. By embracing these AI-powered analytical tools, you are positioning yourself to make more informed decisions, respond quicker to changing conditions, and identify opportunities that otherwise might go unnoticed. The future of business decision-making is here, and it is augmented by AI.

OTHER INDUSTRY-SPECIFIC TOOLS

One of the most significant benefits of industry-specific AI tools is their ability to improve efficiency and reduce costs. As routine tasks are automated, human resources are freed for more strategic work. In industries such as healthcare and legal services, where documentation and compliance are critical, AI-driven tools significantly reduce administrative burdens. Similarly, in logistics and retail, real-time data analysis allows businesses to adapt quickly to changing conditions, improving their operations.

Implementing AI in an operational company brings significant change, especially for small and medium businesses. While large companies are investing in these tools with near-limitless budgets, smaller organizations need to be more objective on how they will leverage the technology. Many of these are built on top of LLMs, and it is those specialized to cater to specific industry needs by offering tailored solutions that the impact can be seen. By improving efficiency, decreasing costs, and enhancing customer satisfaction, many of these companies can compete with larger organizations with heftier investments.

Here are 10 examples for you to consider:

- **Healthcare:** Clinical documentation management tools such as Dragon Medical One leverage LLMs to transcribe doctor–patient interactions in real time. These tools reduce the burden of paperwork on healthcare professionals by automating note-taking, allowing them to focus more on patient care. Additionally, with these tools, you can ensure accuracy in medical records and improve compliance with industry regulations. Automating routine tasks ultimately allows for these professionals to save time, increase diagnosis and treatment rates, and reduce administrative costs.
- **Education:** Many examples could be named for adaptive learning platforms that can be leveraged in education. Tools such as ScribeSense use LLMs to personalize the learning experience for students and streamline educator work by analyzing performance data and adjusting content delivery accordingly. By using the correct prompts, you could provide tailored lesson plans and exercises, ensuring that students receive support based on their learning pace and style. For schools and organizations dedicated to learning practices, tools such as these can reduce teacher workload and improve student outcomes.
- **Logistics:** Tools such as Wise System can help optimize delivery routes by analyzing traffic patterns, weather conditions, and package constraints as they are being delivered. Using these tools allows the company to reduce fuel costs and improve

delivery time, ultimately leading to customer satisfaction. Companies can benefit from this application in logistics and transportation to manage fleets more efficiently and deliver with fewer resources. Companies such as FedEx and UPS have already started implementing tools such as these to manage their vehicles, obtaining significant results since doing so.

- **Legal services:** Legal research and document review tools like Casetext's CoCounsel use LLMs to analyze large volumes of legal documents quickly and accurately. These tools can identify relevant case law, draft legal memos, and even spot inconsistencies in contracts. For small law firms, these tools reduce time spent on research and improve accuracy, enabling more clients to be served without increasing costs or hiring more personnel.

- **Retail:** Popular retailers are turning to AI-powered marketing assistants, such as Phrasee, to create personalized email campaigns and social media posts. Tools such as these analyze customer behavior data and generate content that will resonate with the desired audience according to their characteristics, needs, and demands. From increased customer engagement to higher conversion rates, these companies usually see increased profits and a stronger community without the need for large marketing teams or hefty advertising investments.

- **Sports:** One of the most popular applications of LLMs is in the sports industry, with applications such as Zone7 being used to analyze player performance data to predict injuries and recommend training adjustments. Large datasets are processed from wearable devices and training logs, which you will often see players use underneath their jerseys or wrapped around their arms. These tools allow coaches and training staff to analyze performance and make data-driven decisions. This proves to be a critical application of the technology, especially since coaches can create targeted performance analytics to improve athlete outcomes and reduce costly injury-related downtime.

- **Real estate:** Property valuation tools such as Zillow's Zestimate use AI technology and ML algorithms to provide accurate property price estimates. These tools analyze historical sales data, market trends, and property features to predict fair market values. Additionally, by leveraging LLMs for this purpose, realtors can improve decision-making when buying or selling properties and enhance client trust by offering data-backed insights. Although these tools can be used by larger organizations, they can also be leveraged by smaller companies and real estate agents to gain a competitive edge and remain aligned with market practices and expectations.

- **Human resources:** AI and LLMs have been increasingly adopted in the human resources business, helping companies analyze resumes and matching them with job descriptions and openings. This is the case of platforms such as Eightfold AI, which uses the technology to match candidates to open positions and predict their success on the job. Other capacities tools such as these often include a comprehensive analysis to suggest upskilling opportunities and professional enhancement. Finally, HR and recruitment areas can benefit from AI by reducing hiring time, improving candidate fit, and enhancing employee retention.

- **Financial services:** Financial firms are leveraging tools like ThetaRay for anti-money laundering and fraud detection. Tools such as these analyze transaction data to identify suspicious patterns and flag potential compliance risks. As real-time analysis and monitoring are implemented, there are reduced regulatory risks for these organizations, ensuring they remain compliant without hiring large compliance teams.

- **Agriculture:** Tools such as Granular are helping farmers make data-driven decisions about planting, irrigation, and harvesting. These tools analyze weather data, solid conditions, and crop health to optimize yields and costs. By associating AI technology with satellite images and incredible processing power as conditions change, you can increase productivity and profitability by adopting precision farming techniques without hiring large teams or needing a lot of resources and by having an all-in-one approach to decision-making.

While these AI tools offer several benefits, it is also important to consider the challenges they may pose. Some of these include implementation costs, data privacy concerns, and the need for human oversight, as often stated. It is also crucial to ensure that these AI tools are ethically used and free from bias, especially in areas that deal with sensitive information, requiring the need for a balance between leveraging technology and maintaining ethical practices.

As you explore these different applications, it is natural that you have doubts about other uses and applications in your business. For these reasons, in the final section of this chapter, you will read about case studies, applications, and prompts you can use for diverse purposes. As you will see, it is only a matter of starting—once you get the hang of it, you will be able to unleash the full power of AI tools within your professional life.

CASE STUDIES AND APPLICATIONS

Successfully implementing LLMs in the industry you work for will depend on how these tools will be leveraged. By understanding how larger companies have incorporated them into their businesses, you can obtain a road map that will help you find the best alternatives for your organization. In this final section of the chapter, you will explore how these versatile tools are being applied to solve specific challenges and lessons learned from their experiences. Additionally, you will see different prompt examples that might help you achieve similar results in your own business.

Case Study 1: eBay

eBay developed a framework that integrates different AI models to assist its staff in coding and marketing tasks. This system automates complex processes, enhancing operational efficiency. Using AI, eBay streamlined operations, allowing the company to handle tasks more efficiently and allocate human resources to strategic initiatives (Lin, 2025). eBay saw that integrating AI models into the business to automate complex tasks is feasible, but human oversight remains essential to ensure alignment with business objectives and handle nuanced scenarios.

Prompt example: "Generate a product description for a vintage 1960s jacket, highlighting its unique features and appeal to fashion enthusiasts."

Case Study 2: HubSpot

HubSpot introduced an AI-powered content creation tool to help marketers generate blog posts, social media content, and email campaigns quickly. By inputting a brief description, users can generate high-quality search engine optimization (SEO) content. The tool helped marketers increase content production by 40% while maintaining quality (Bodiroza, 2023). It also reduced time spent on first drafts, allowing teams to focus on strategy and refinement.

Prompt example: "Write a 500-word blog post on the benefits of email marketing for small businesses."

Case Study 3: Johnson & Johnson

Johnson & Johnson uses AI to enhance its drug discovery process, specifically in optimizing chemical synthesis. These models automate complex tasks, streamlining the development of new pharmaceuticals. With its implementation, it could now speed up the drug development process, enabling the company to bring new medication to the market more efficiently (Lin, 2025). When pharmaceutical companies can implement these programs in their processes, it allows for a more nuanced and monitored activity, ensuring they operate within the desired parameters and contribute effectively to research objectives.

Prompt example: "Develop an AI-driven strategy to optimize chemical synthesis processes in pharmaceutical research, focusing on reducing time and resource consumption."

Case Study 4: Cosentino

The Spanish brand Cosentino adopted AI to create agents that operate as a digital workforce to manage customer orders and operational tasks. These agents autonomously handle functions such as credit management, processing blocked orders, and enabling credit managers to process up to five times more orders without additional risk. This adoption led to increased operational efficiency, allowing humans to focus on more strategic business areas (Lin, 2025). When companies treat AI as digital employees with complete foundational skills, it becomes easier to adhere to company processes and compliance standards.

Prompt example: "Design an AI agent to autonomously manage customer order processing in a manufacturing company, ensuring compliance with credit policies and enhancing operational efficiency."

Case Study 5: Best Buy

The retail company partnered with Google to develop an AI-powered virtual assistant to help customers with self-service options. The idea is for the assistant to help customers troubleshoot product issues, modify order deliveries and schedules, and manage subscriptions. The company wants customers and human customer care agents to have AI-enabled tools that will help with real-time assistance, analyzing customer interactions, offering relevant recommendations, summarizing sentiment, and using call data to prevent future issues (Tilzer,

2024). Companies are implementing these solutions to ensure that there is a more personalized and efficient customer support experience, as well as streamline operations and allow employees to focus on complex customer needs.

Prompt example: "Design a generative AI-driven virtual assistant for a retail company that can handle customer inquiries, manage orders, and provide personalized product recommendations."

Other Useful Prompts

Here are 10 useful prompts you might want to consider using depending on your industry:

- **Marketing:** "Generate a 500-word blog post that explains the benefits of using social media marketing for small businesses. Ensure the tone is professional yet approachable, include three specific examples, and suggest a call-to-action at the end."
- **Sales:** "Write a personalized cold email for a B2B SaaS company offering project management software. Address the recipient's pain points of collaboration inefficiency and suggest a free demo. Keep the email concise, persuasive, and under 200 words."
- **Customer support:** "Create a professional response template for a customer service team addressing delayed product shipments. Apologize sincerely, explain potential causes briefly, and offer a discount code as compensation."
- **HR:** "Draft a job description for a Senior Data Analyst role. Include required skills (e.g., SQL, Python, and data visualization), experience (5+ years), and a brief description of the company culture."
- **Finance:** "Summarize the key financial metrics of a quarterly earnings report, including revenue, profit margin, and year-

over-year growth. Provide a brief analysis highlighting significant trends or concerns."

- **Legal:** "Analyze the following nondisclosure agreement and highlight any clauses that may present legal risks for a small startup. Suggest modifications if necessary."
- **Education:** "Design a 60-minute lesson plan for a high school history class about the Industrial Revolution. Include a brief lecture outline, an interactive activity, and discussion questions to encourage critical thinking."
- **Product development:** "Based on the following user feedback, prioritize three new features for a mobile banking app. Justify the selection using criteria such as user demand, implementation complexity, and potential impact."
- **Logistics:** "Suggest an optimal delivery route for a logistics company with 10 drop-off points in a metropolitan area. Assume traffic data and delivery time windows are critical factors."
- **Real estate:** "Write a compelling property listing for a 3-bedroom, 2-bathroom suburban house. Highlight key selling points, such as a recently renovated kitchen, proximity to schools, and a large backyard."

Using these prompts as examples and adjusting them to your business, you will be able to start practicing and seeing the results that the LLM will provide you. However, while understanding and implementing AI tools is a significant step, the real potential lies in turning innovative ideas into sustainable income streams.

In the next chapter, you will understand how professionals and entrepreneurs are making money with AI by creatively leveraging these tools. Whether you are aiming to create a passive income stream, launch a new business, or enhance an existing one, the following two chapters will guide you through the practical steps of transforming AI-driven innovation into profitable ventures.

TURNING IDEAS INTO INCOME

As you might imagine, AI has created unprecedented opportunities for entrepreneurs and professionals to transform their expertise and ideas into successful businesses. Unlike previous technological revolutions, AI tools are unique since they allow you to amplify your capabilities. This usually means delivering higher-quality services and solving complex problems more efficiently.

In this chapter, you will see some of the practical steps of leveraging AI tools to create active income streams. You will see why AI is such an incredible opportunity for new business ventures, and how it can be used to enhance your services or create new ones. As you read, you will find different business models that are well-suited for AI integration, from consulting services to specialized solutions for specific industries.

Through real-world case studies, you will see how others have successfully built AI-enhanced businesses and examine the strategies used to overcome challenges. Whether you are a professional looking to start a side business or an entrepreneur ready to launch a full-scale venture, you will obtain all the information you need to build your own business and achieve financial success. Are you ready to discover how?

WHY USE AI FOR A NEW OPPORTUNITY?

While many might discuss the negative implications of AI in the market today, others are using this opportunity of an evolving market to leverage the technology to their advantage. With LLMs becoming more accessible to the market and easier to work with, they have become a powerful ally for those who want to look at new opportunities. Along with their increasingly enhancing features and capabilities, more people are resorting to these models to help them move out of the ordinary and bring new value to businesses.

AI is an incredible tool that can help entrepreneurs and professionals achieve success in areas never imagined before. Its capacity to generate new ideas and to interact with a human with the machine's processing capability allowed it to transform the business environment in revolutionary ways. *But can AI really help me develop new opportunities and increase my income?* Yes, and not only this, but it can help you turn that idea that was left inside the drawer into a real income stream if used correctly.

Here are eight reasons to start using AI LLMs as soon as you close this book:

- **Scale and efficiency:** AI's ability to handle massive amounts of data and automate tasks creates opportunities that traditional exclusively human-operating businesses cannot match. Consider a solo entrepreneur who recently adopted an AI-powered legal document review service or an accountant who subscribed to accounting software that recognizes invoices. By leveraging AI, they can analyze hundreds of contracts and documents at the same time, offering a high-level service at a fraction of traditional costs. This kind of scale would usually require a team of professionals, but AI enables a single professional to deliver equivalent or better results.

- **Personalization at scale:** One of AI's most powerful aspects is its ability to provide personalized experiences without the traditional trade-off between customization and scalability. Suppose you are a fitness instructor who uses an AI-powered platform that creates individually tailored workout programs based on each user's fitness level, goals, available equipment, and even daily energy levels. The system would adapt in real time to user feedback and progress, providing a level of personalization that would be impossible for a human professional to maintain across thousands of clients.

- **Innovative problem-solving approach:** Solving traditional problems is sometimes easier when you adopt AI into your workflow. In this case, you can imagine an urban farmer who adopted an AI program to optimize their indoor growing conditions. The system allows them to monitor traditional metrics like humidity and temperature, analyze plant growth patterns through computer analysis, predict crop yields, and adjust growing conditions to maximize production. This level of precision and automation allows urban farming to be economically feasible in spaces previously unsuited for agriculture.

- **Market gap identification:** In the past, companies used to carry out extensive market research to identify new market opportunities and identify the potential of new products. With AI, marketers and researchers can identify untapped opportunities by analyzing vast amounts of data to spot patterns and trends. In this case, a social media analyst could use AI to analyze conversations and online reviews across multiple industries to identify specific pain points that were not being addressed by existing solutions. A successful venture would lead to the development of a widely accepted niche product that larger companies might have overlooked.

- **Enhanced decision-making:** As you have seen in previous chapters, AI's ability to analyze large volumes of data allows professionals to have greater insight than would be impossible through traditional methods. In this case, a realtor who adopted AI into their work processes would be able to analyze hundreds of factors that affect the value of a property, from social media sentiment to satellite images showing neighborhood changes. This would allow them to identify up-and-coming areas before property prices rise and allow for more informed investment decisions and higher returns.

- **Rapid prototype and testing:** Another advantage of AI programs, especially LLMs, is that they accelerate the product development cycle by allowing rapid testing and idea iteration. In this case, you can carry out a "conversation" with the machine and refine ideas until the optimal solution is reached. Professionals in the fashion industry, for example, could use AI to generate and test thousands of designs and products with variations and gather feedback through virtual try-ons without producing any physical items. This process helps reduce waste, cut costs, and ensures a better market fit for their products, ultimately increasing profits and revenue.

- **Creating new value from existing resources:** Due to its ability to analyze and identify patterns invisible to the human eye, AI models can extract value from existing assets or data that were previously hidden. Business consultants, for example, could subscribe to an AI app that would analyze a client's historical business data to identify operational inefficiencies and growth opportunities that at first were not visible through traditional analysis. This could open up new opportunities and revenue streams from data the business already had but was not fully used to its best advantage.

- **Removal of barriers to market entry:** In many markets, the most frequent barrier faced by professionals is the need to have expertise and experience to work in it. However, with AI, the need for these, and even resources, has significantly reduced, allowing professionals with less experience to remove the initial barriers. Translators, for example, could use specialized translation services for medical documents, combining AI's speed with human expertise for the final check. This hybrid approach allows them to compete with larger translation services while maintaining high accuracy and lower costs.

The opportunity to create value with AI is not just about using the technology; it is also about identifying where the technology can solve real problems in real ways. To successfully leverage these tools, professionals must focus on value creation, identifying specific problems where AI can provide unique solutions and add value. Similarly, it is essential to start with clear use cases, meaning there must be well-defined problems that AI is suited to solve and that will build on the expertise you have in the industry.

At the same time, while implementing AI to generate new income is not uncommon, precautions must be taken to ensure it is a profitable venture. This means, for example maintaining the human connection with clients and using the technology to augment rather than replace your expertise. Generally, hybrid solutions offer customers a higher level of comfort, especially for those who are more resistant to change. Finally, you must remain adaptable and be prepared to evolve your approach as AI capabilities advance. Continuously learn and adjust your business model based on market feedback and the changes that happen in the market.

BUSINESS OPPORTUNITIES WITH LLMS

Whether you are looking to start a side business or launch a full-time venture, LLMs can help you create valuable services that meet real market needs. This section will explore real-life implementations of how technology can significantly change the way you work and generate income. Read on to discover 10 ways you can use AI and LLMs for a business opportunity:

- Sarah, a language teacher, transformed her traditional tutoring business by incorporating AI tools. She now offers personalized language learning experiences that were previously impossible to scale. With the use of LLMs, she can generate custom lesson plans and track student progress while focusing on providing high-value guidance and conversation practice. As a result, her students progress faster, and she can charge premium rates for this enhanced service.

- Marcus used LLMs to build a consulting practice, associating his knowledge with the tool's capabilities. He helps businesses analyze their content performance across platforms, predict trending topics, and create data-driven content calendars. What sets his service apart is how he uses AI to process market data while applying his human insight to craft strategies that resonate with specific audiences.

- Elena launched a modern career coaching service that goes beyond traditional resume writing. By using AI-enhanced systems, she optimizes professional documents for specific industries, while providing personalized coaching on interview techniques and career strategy. The combination of AI efficiency and human experience allowed her to help more clients and charge above market values for the insights that human knowledge associated with technology capacity offers.

- David used AI to enter the world of small business analytics, something that was before the domain of large firms. He created a service that helps small businesses understand their customers' behaviors, predict inventory needs, and optimize pricing strategies. By automating the data analysis process, he can offer sophisticated insights at prices that small businesses can afford and increase his customer base and income.

- Patricia's innovative approach to event planning by using AI took her business to another level. She developed an AI-enhanced service that generates creative event concepts and optimizes venue layouts. Additionally, the program helps her predict attendance patterns, offering significant savings to her clients and allowing them to cut costs. This technical edge allows her to create more memorable events while managing resources more efficiently.

- Dr. Chen found a different niche to work within the academic world. By leveraging AI tools, he helps researchers enhance their scientific papers by improving paper structure, checking methodology consistency, and generating compelling visual aids. What started as a side project for alternate income grew into a full-time business serving researchers worldwide.

- James, a real estate entrepreneur, started to adopt AI to provide services that go beyond market analysis. By using these systems, he can predict neighborhood trends, estimate renovation costs, and generate rental income forecasts. This approach allowed him to increase his client base and expand the market he works in, making him a valued advisor to property investors.

- Michelle, a writer, found that with the help of AI tools, she can enhance her creative writing workshop services. She uses LLMs to generate unique story prompts, analyze plot structures, and provide character development insights while offering personal mentoring to help writers develop their craft. Associating technology and personal guidance allowed her to create a unique learning experience that writers are eager to join.

- Carlos is an independent consultant in the sports business and uses AI to enhance player performance. As he combined his knowledge with technology, he was able to analyze player movement and generate personalized training programs. His service helps athletes optimize their performance while minimizing injury risks, creating value that traditional coaching alone would not provide.

The key to success in any of these ventures is not just about leveraging the right AI tools, but also understanding how the technology can be combined with human expertise to enhance services and create something truly valuable. When you are looking for the same opportunities for yourself, start by identifying areas where you have domain knowledge and can meaningfully enhance traditional approaches with AI capabilities. Focus on building scalable systems while maintaining quality by using your expertise.

Finally, you must also remember to price your services strategically, considering the value you provide, the market's willingness to pay, and the costs that you have associated with the business. Offer tiered service levels that allow clients to choose the level of support they need, and always include premium options for those who want service at the highest level. The opportunity to create value with AI is fast and growing. Reflecting on all probabilities will allow you to build a sustainable business that serves clients while providing you with rewarding work and financial returns.

REAL-WORLD CASE STUDIES

In the previous section, you saw some examples of how AI can be leveraged in different industries. However, while these are merely fictional examples to show that technology can be associated with your profession, some businesses and companies are already using them in the real world. Let's explore five examples of where the association between LLMs and humans in business has proven to be a success and led to corporate transformation.

- **Nakie** produces hammocks from recycled materials and faced a challenge as demand for its eco-friendly products increased. By adopting an AI-driven inventory management powered by LLMs, the company automated its supply chain operations, ensuring that stock levels were always optimized based on real-time demand forecasts. This technology enabled the company to manage a growing product line while reducing manual workload. As a result, it improved order accuracy, reduced stockouts, and scaled its operations without a significant increase in staff, maintaining its competitive edge in the market (Boyer, 2024).

- **Sprinklr** is a medium-sized social media management platform that offers services to enterprise clients. It adopted LLMs to enhance its social media listening and sentiment analysis capabilities. With AI models capable of processing huge amounts of data, it provided customers with real-time insights into customer behavior and emerging trends. This allows marketing teams to make data-driven decisions and tailor their campaigns more effectively. Doing so allowed the company to increase its product offering and strengthened client retention by delivering more precise and actionable intelligence (ODSC - Open Data Science, 2023).

- **Randy Speckman Design** is a boutique design agency that uses AI-powered tools to automate content creation for client proposals, presentations, and marketing collateral. In the company's systems, AI handles routine tasks like drafting design briefs and generating ideas, while employees focus on creative execution and client interaction. This adoption of the technology allowed the firm to deliver high-quality projects faster while keeping operational costs low. As a result, it expanded its client base and increased revenue without needing to hire additional staff (Anderson, 2024).

- **CMY Cubes**, a small business offering interactive science, technology, engineering, arts, and math toys, leveraged a custom-built GPT-powered tool to supercharge its content marketing strategy. It automated the generation of SEO-friendly blog posts, product descriptions, and social media content, achieving significant cost savings and improving its online visibility. The AI model also provided actionable insights by analyzing customer feedback and performance data, helping the company optimize its marketing campaigns.

As a result, there was a significant increase in organic traffic and customer engagement, boosting sales and increasing revenue (Boyer, 2024).

- **Notice Ninja** is a tech-driven business offering tax compliance solutions that faced challenges managing the constant changes in tax regulations. The issue was solved when they integrated AI-enabled tools based on LLMs to automate key processes like document review, compliance checks, and reporting, leading to reduced human error, accelerated turnaround times, and improved client satisfaction. Additionally, the AI allowed the company to handle a larger client base without compromising service quality, leading to increased revenue and market share (Anderson, 2024).

These success stories demonstrate that AI is not just for large companies with massive budgets. Strategically implementing AI into your company can transform your business, regardless of its size. The lesson that should remain here is that successful AI integration requires a clear understanding of business needs, careful tool selection, and a commitment to learning and adaptation. These companies did not just adopt AI for its own sake; they identified specific challenges and found ways to leverage tools to solve them effectively.

At the same time, while these stories are inspiring, they also raise important questions about responsible AI monetization. As you consider your own AI-powered business ventures, it is crucial to understand how to create sustainable revenue streams while maintaining ethical practices. Read on to explore how you can use AI and still generate profit and contribute positively to society, maintaining long-term viability for the business.

ETHICAL AND SUSTAINABLE AI MONETIZATION STRATEGIES

As professionals and entrepreneurs find new ways to leverage AI to enhance their businesses, the questions regarding ethical and sustainable concerns are growing at the same level. Responsible AI use is not just a question of doing what is right; it is essential for long-term trust, sustainability, and growth. As you explore some of the considerations to keep in mind, remember that the AI world encompasses much more than this, which will be further explored in Chapter 9.

Transparency

For any business leveraging AI, trust is invaluable. Customers want to know how AI is being used, what data is being collected, and whether human oversight is present. Being transparent about your AI operations creates a sense of accountability and builds trust with users, meaning it is not enough to offer the latest technology. You must also clearly communicate how AI powers your service, if and why personal data is being collected, the known limitations of the model, and where humans are involved.

Responsible Data Use

As you know, AI models are powered by data, and without access to these datasets, the models cannot deliver accurate and meaningful results. However, it is the business's job to ensure that data collection and handling is done responsibly to ensure user trust. You must adopt clear policies on data collection, use, and storage, including giving users control over what they provide. This might mean offering opt-in or opt-out choices, access to account data, and maintaining strict security protocols to prevent breaches.

Addressing Bias and Ensuring Fairness

When AI systems are trained on biased data, they can produce discriminatory or unfair outcomes. These have consequences in daily life, meaning that when adopting these tools, you must test the model periodically for unintended biases, ensure diverse and representative training sets, and create feedback mechanisms that allow users to report unfair behavior. By prioritizing fairness, you can mitigate risk and appeal to more customers, as they will trust the content you are providing.

Minimizing Environmental Footprint

Environmental costs are one of the most significant when considering AI use, especially due to the significant amount of energy that is consumed during the training and deployment phases. Businesses must adopt sustainability as a key part of their strategy, choosing energy-efficient models, optimizing AI operations to minimize waste, using green hosting solutions powered by renewable energy, and offsetting carbon footprints by investing in environmental projects, where possible, to stand out in an increasingly sustainability-driven market.

Developing Customer-Centric Solutions

The last consideration is that while AI can be a valuable tool, you must ensure that it is not only about automating tasks and enhancing efficiency. You should look for AI implementation where it genuinely improves the customer experience and solves real problems rather than creating unnecessary complexities or removing all human inter-action. This connection must be enhanced, and not replaced, including offering human assistance when needed and regularly collecting user feedback to improve AI interaction. Doing so will allow you to enhance user satisfaction and differentiate your business from competitors that are only looking for automation and cost reduction.

It is also essential to keep up-to-date with ethical guidelines and best practices, ensuring your business is adaptable to the changes in the market. This can mean staying informed about new developments, industry standards, and regulatory changes. Creating an ethical AI framework should not be something that is done once, but an ongoing process that is regularly updated and reviewed.

As you move forward, it is time to explore the other side of AI businesses that will require little to no input from your side: earning passive income. From automated content creation to AI-driven affiliate marketing and digital product sales, you will see some strategies to generate revenue with minimum hands-on effort. Are you ready to learn how to turn into A self-sustaining engine of profit? Keep on going to find out how!

BUILDING AN AI-POWERED BUSINESS

It is not uncommon to find individuals who are looking for different ways to earn an extra income but struggle to find the time. Between demanding jobs, family responsibilities, and personal commitments, there is little room left to start a side hustle or new venture. This is where AI comes in: It does not only need to be used for income sources you will work with, like you have seen in the previous chapter. It also offers solutions for those seeking to generate passive income with minimal ongoing efforts. With LLMs and AI, creating tools that work for you even as you sleep is possible!

From developing automated products and services to building digital solutions that require little maintenance, you can find an AI solution that will help you achieve this goal. Among the options are automated content creation, AI customer-driven support, and selling customized AI tools, all within a few strokes on the keyboard. To help you understand this process, this chapter will help you see the alternatives to launching your own AI-powered business.

You will also explore open-source LLMs that can be tailored to fit specific niches, giving you more control and creativity in your business model. Also within this chapter are insights into potential challenges and pitfalls, which you must be aware of so they can be addressed effectively. If you are looking for a new way to grow your income without sacrificing your time, AI offers exciting solutions that will help you turn time constraints into financial freedom.

USING AI FOR PASSIVE INCOME

One of the main advantages of integrating AI into business ventures is that the model will do most of the heavy lifting while you collect on top of its success. Regardless of the industry applying it to, those looking for extra income will find that knowing how to leverage these tools will open up new—and even multiple—opportunities for some extra cash at the end of the month. The best part is that once the business model is designed, they can let the technology handle most of the work, requiring minimal input.

- **Automated content creation:** Using LLMs to create content allows you to reduce the time required to create content from hours to just a few minutes. You can use AI tools to generate articles, schedule posts, and even respond to comments. You can even create a monetized blog or YouTube channel using AI-generated content, allowing you to earn from revenue, affiliate links, or sponsored content.
    - *Example:* Some entrepreneurs use AI to run niche blogs on topics like travel, technology, or fitness. Once the AI produces high-quality posts, the blog earns passive income through ads and affiliate programs.
- **Affiliate marketing:** AI can also be used to supercharge your strategy of earning money by promoting other people's products and earning a commission on sales. LLMs will allow you to create targeted content faster, identify high-converting products, and optimize marketing campaigns. Strategies like using driven keyword analyzers and content generators can significantly enhance the process.

- *Example:* An affiliate marketer could use AI to build a website focused on reviewing tech gadgets. With AI generating product reviews and optimizing SEO, the site can consistently drive traffic and passive income without requiring constant attention.
- **Subscription-based services:** Another lucrative passive income stream you can benefit from is offering AI-powered subscription-based services. These could include chatbots, AI financial advisors, and other tasks that can be automated. Once developed, customers pay a recurring fee to access these services, generating consistent revenue.
    - *Example:* You can create an AI-powered writing assistant tailored for legal professionals. Once the tool is built and marketed, it could continue generating passive income through monthly or annual subscriptions.
- **Stock analysis tools:** If you are interested in finance, it might interest you to know that you can create an AI-driven stock analysis tool to generate passive income. These programs use ML algorithms to predict stock trends and offer investment insights to companies and traders. You can earn money from these tools through subscription services or premium access to advanced features.
    - *Example:* Financial entrepreneurs developed AI platforms that analyze market data and provide automated trading signals. Once users subscribe to these platforms, the owner earns a steady income.
- **Chatbots for businesses:** Commonly used for customer support, lead generation, and user engagement, AI tools also allow you to build chatbots specific to certain industries. Once they are ready, you can license them out for recurring fees and even create subscription tiers. Since the chatbots operate 24/7, they will provide consistent value with little maintenance.
    - *Example:* You can develop a chatbot that is specifically designed for real estate agents. The bot can handle

inquiries, schedule viewings, and answer common questions. The tool could be offered on a subscription basis and generate passive income.

- **Online courses:** Education today is widely accessible, and you can automate the full process of course development with AI tools. This means creating the content, posting updates, grading activities, and even setting personalized tutoring. Other possibilities are course material, quizzes, and interactive content, reducing the manual workload. Once the course is live, income can come from course sales, subscriptions, and certificates.
    - *Example:* A teacher could use AI to create a series of courses on their subject of expertise. They would use the tool to automate most of the development and the delivery process, ensuring that passive income is generated long after the initial launch. As a bonus, they could also use AI to translate the content and sell or caption it in other languages.
- **Ecommerce stores:** AI can help run automated ecommerce stores by managing inventory, setting prices, and even handling customer service. With tools that predict demand and optimize pricing strategies, you can minimize your involvement while maximizing profits.
    - *Example:* Online store owners today use AI-driven tools to print-on-demand businesses such as customized T-shirts and products. The AI manages product listings, optimizes ads, and handles customer interactions, leaving the owner to do little beyond the occasional oversight.
- **Licensing AI models:** If you have the technical skills to develop your own AI models, licensing them to other businesses can generate passive income. For example, you might create a model that predicts customer churn or optimizes supply chain operations and license it to companies in relevant industries.

○ *Example:* A developer builds an AI model that helps retailers predict inventory needs. After licensing it to multiple businesses, they earn recurring fees for its usage.

- **Social media management:** For many businesses, social media management is a time-consuming task. However, with AI, this process can be streamlined and significantly simplified. Using AI tools, you can create a social media scheduler or content generator and charge a monthly fee for using your tool.
  ○ *Example:* Some marketing companies are working with platforms that generate and schedule posts based on trending topics. Once businesses sign up, you will have an active business in which AI handles most of the work.

- **Virtual assistants:** AI-powered virtual personal assistants can help individuals manage their daily tasks, such as scheduling meetings, setting reminders, and managing emails. You could create a subscription service that would monetize the work and bring you extra income.
  ○ *Example:* Some startups have created virtual assistants specifically designed for entrepreneurs. Once users subscribe, the AI handles repetitive tasks, providing value while generating income for the creator.

As you can see, there are numerous ways to generate passive income with AI, and it will all depend on your creativity! The key is identifying a niche or area where AI can deliver real value and create systems requiring minimal maintenance. To help you understand this development process and how to achieve the best outcomes, the guide you will see next will be the road map for your future ventures.

ROAD MAP TO CREATING AN AI-POWERED BUSINESS

Starting an AI-powered business requires diligence and a systematic approach that balances technological capabilities with market needs. Here is a road map to help you determine if the business you are considering is a good fit and the steps you will need to take to increase the chances of success.

1. **Identify and validate market problems:** Identify the specific pain points or inefficiencies that your LLM will target. Focus on problems where humanlike text processing, analysis, or generation could create significant value. Validate your identified problem through direct conversations with potential customers, online research of industry forums and communities, analysis of existing solutions and their limitations, and surveys or interviews with industry specialists.

2. **Define your value proposition:** In a document, clearly articulate how your AI solution will solve the identified problem better than the existing alternatives. The value proposition should include the specific business outcome you want to achieve, offer measurable improvements (time saved, cost reduced, quality improved), be easily understandable by nontechnical stakeholders, and differentiate your solution from conventional approaches.

3. **Develop a business model:** Define how your AI solution will generate revenue. This could mean it is a subscription product for ongoing access, usage-based pricing for specific operations, enterprise licensing for larger deployments, and hybrid models combining different pricing approaches. You will need to know exactly what the business you are developing is to identify the later characteristics of the tool and build it accordingly.

4. **Select your technical stack:** Carry out the necessary research and choose the best tools and technologies based on your requirements. This process should include looking at API solutions for quick deployment and scalability, cloud infrastructure providers, development frameworks and libraries for AI integration, and the technologies that will be used for your application. **Note:** For many of the existing tools

today, such as GPT, you will need minimal technical intervention to create an app. You must also remember to verify the cost structure and pricing models, technical capabilities and limitations, integration requirements, and data privacy and security needs.

5. **Build a minimum viable product (MVP):** Create a basic working prototype that demonstrates what you are offering to the market. The MVP should focus on one core function that solves the main problem, has basic error handling and user feedback mechanisms integrated, offers an intuitive and user-friendly interface, and includes analytics to track usage and performance metrics.

6. **Test and iterate with users:** Find and engage early adopters to validate your solution. This can include 5–10 potential users willing to test the prototype and create a structured feedback collection process. It is also important to focus on monitoring the key metrics like usage patterns and error rates and document your findings, common issues, and user suggestions.

7. **Address technical and ethical considerations:** Ensure your solution is built responsibly. This means implementing proper data handling and privacy measures, considering bias and fairness in the implementation, developing transparent policies about AI use, and planning for model updates, reviews, and maintenance.

8. **Create a go-to-market strategy:** Plan how you will launch the product into the market by identifying initial target segments and developing marketing messages that resonate with the audience. You should also remember to create educational content about your AI solution and build partnerships with industry influencers or complementary businesses to ensure increased engagement and reach.

9. **Prepare for scaling:** Plan for the tool to grow and increase use in the future. This means you must take into account technical infrastructure scalability, customer support

processes, documentation and training materials, and team expansion needs. The tool must have all its information documented to ensure that others can consult information if necessary.

10. **Establish success metrics:** Finally, define key performance metrics (KPIs) that are relevant to the business you are developing. These include user adoption and retention rates, customer satisfaction scores, technical performance metrics, and financial indicators.

During the process, especially if you are new to managing these tools, it is normal and acceptable to feel frustrated. If this happens, you must remember that starting a business is an iterative process, where you will need to start small, focus on solving a specific problem, and continuously gather user feedback. At the same time, as mentioned earlier, several of these tools already come with built-in features that will allow you to integrate them into a website, for example, if necessary.

During the research process, you might be surprised at the cost these tools can come at. Do not feel hindered by this, as there are many options in the market. Some of them are just as powerful as paid tools, and you might not even need premium subscriptions, depending on what you plan to use them for. Regardless of the case, the following section will explore open-source LLM options, which can provide additional flexibility and cost advantages for what you are trying to build.

EXPLORING OPEN-SOURCE LLMS FOR BUSINESS

When thinking about leveraging LLMs, our first reaction is usually to think about ChatGPT. This is only natural, as it was the first tool and still serves, in many ways, as a benchmark for how AI tools would work. However, as you have seen in Chapter 4, the market does not only have licensed AI programs but also a world of open-source language models that could save you a significant amount of cash every month. While recurring to the most widely known tool is usually the first option we resort to, it is important to know there are several others that can help you achieve the same goals at a more reasonable price.

These are called open-source LLMs and include tools such as Llama, Mistral, and BLOOM, all of which represent an interesting alternative to proprietary solutions. Think of these models as customizable engines you can modify to fit your specific business needs. Just as you might customize a vehicle for specific purposes, these models can be tailored to your industry's unique requirements.

But what about technical expertise? you might ask. That is the topic that has probably been on your mind as you are reading these chapters. The good news is that while some technical knowledge helps, it is not always necessary. You can start off with friendly platforms such as Hugging Face's Space platform, which allows you to experiment with AI without writing a single line of code.

The process of building your custom tool will happen in stages. You might begin with prebuilt solutions that require no coding, similar to using a website builder instead of writing the code from scratch. As your needs grow, you could either invest in learning basic technical skills or bring in expertise through hiring or partnerships. Many successful AI businesses started this way, gradually building their technical capabilities as their needs evolved.

The cost–benefit comparison can be alarming. Unlike proprietary solutions that charge per token or API call, open-source models can be run on your own equipment. This is similar to buying a coffee machine instead of paying per cup at a café: There is an upfront investment, but it often pays for itself over time. In some cases, depending on the use and frequency, the cost of using open-source platforms can be as minimal as 10% when compared to tools such as Gemini, ChatGPT, and even Claude.

However, it is the customizability where there is the main difference. Using these models allows you to train the machine to understand your industry's specific jargon, adapt to your brand's voice, or handle specialized tasks. For those starting out, a practical path includes being with hosted solutions that offer user-friendly interfaces. As your understanding grows, you can explore more customized solutions and scale as you continue.

The secret is to match your approach and capabilities while keeping an eye on future needs. You can start with simple applications and gradually increase complexity. As AI tools evolve, it means that AI technology is no longer limited to tech giants or well-funded startups. Small businesses and independent entrepreneurs can now adopt and adapt AI solutions without breaking the bank. As new tools come to the market and others such as Llama mature, they will open up new opportunities for all kinds of businesses.

Nonetheless, this does not mean that the process will be without its challenges. There might be some, and you must be ready to tackle them head on to ensure that you can continue with your project. When you are informed about the obstacles that might be in the way of increasing your income, it makes it easier to manage the difficulties and prepare for what you have to do next.

CHALLENGES TO EXPECT

As someone looking to build a passive income stream with AI, you should keep in mind that you will face challenges that need careful consideration. While the rewards can be significant, it is important to know the elements that might hinder the process. Knowing these potential obstacles in advance will help you plan and execute your AI business more effectively and understand that if you do face difficulties, it is a part of the learning curve, not a reason to feel frustrated.

Here are eight of the most common challenges faced by those who are starting out in the AI business:

- **Technical complexity and infrastructure:** Even with today's user-friendly tools, you will need to manage the technical aspects of your system. Focus on solutions that automate as much of the technical aspect as possible, allowing you to maintain your passive income stream without constant intervention.
- **Need for human oversight:** While the goal is to create passive income, some level of human oversight remains necessary. Plan for periodic reviews of your AI's performance and regular quality checks. As you establish efficient monitoring processes, ensure that these don't demand too much of your time while ensuring your service maintains high standards.
- **Dataset challenges:** Your AI system will need quality data to perform well. As a small operator, you may face challenges in accessing or creating suitable datasets. Consider starting in niches where publicly available data is accessible and vast or in those where you can gradually build your own dataset during the operation.
- **Model customization and performance:** Getting your AI to perform exactly as needed for your specific use case will take time and effort. While the initial period will be active rather than passive, investing this time upfront can lead to more automated operations later.
- **Technical expertise requirements:** You do not need to become an AI expert, but you will need enough understanding to make informed business decisions. Focus on learning the essential aspects that directly impact your specific application while leveraging existing tools and platforms for more complex tasks.
- **Staying competitive:** The AI field moves quickly, and your passive income stream could dry up if you don't stay current. Carry out regular market research and updates to your system. The goal is to create a business that is sustainable with minimal intervention while remaining competitive.

- **Managing client expectations:** Clear communication about what your AI service can and cannot do will save you time and headaches later. Set up automated systems for managing client expectations and handling common questions or issues.
- **Cost management:** Start with solutions that have predictable costs and clear scaling paths. Your goal is to maintain healthy profit margins while keeping the business as automated as possible. Consider starting with lower-cost options and reinvesting profits as you grow.

The path to creating passive income streams with AI requires careful planning and initial setup, but with the right approach, you can build a sustainable automated business. While complete passivity might be challenging to achieve, you can create a system that runs smoothly with minimal oversight. Still, this does not mean there aren't other constraints you will need to face that could impact your AI business. These include data privacy and security, AI bias and fairness, and even hallucinations, which we have explored previously but will take a closer look at in the next chapter.

ETHICAL AI AND FUTURE TRENDS

When dealing with AI, it is not enough to present good and functional programs. Ethical considerations must also be addressed, meaning they cannot be optional add-ons, but an elementary factor to the tool's success. As creators, deployers, and users of these programs, it is up to us to use these programs responsibly and ensure that what we bring to the market enhances rather than harms society.

In this chapter, we will explore more on what these considerations are, adding to what you have read about so far in the book. You will also catch a glimpse of what to expect regarding the development of technology. If you are worried about technology taking over, rest assured this will not happen in the near future, as you are about to see. The future of AI is promising and exciting, and it will be up to you to know how to best leverage these tools to your advantage.

THE IMPORTANCE OF ETHICAL AI USE

Ethical standards in AI go beyond being transparent about its use and assuming accountability for the information it generates. With an alarmingly high amount of misinformation on the internet today from different channels, it is essential to use this technology responsibly, ensuring that you are not propagating bias or spreading harmful content. The power of AI brings with it considerable ethical responsibilities. Unlike traditional technologies, it can make decisions that affect countless lives in different ways. In the end, it is not *only* about preventing harmful outcomes—it is also about how the future will be shaped so that technology is used for good.

Consider the impact that AI has in our world today: It influences the information we see, the opportunities we are offered, and even how we interact with each other. This significant influence means that we have the responsibility to ensure these systems operate in ways that respect dignity, promote fairness, and protect individual rights. This is not just about compliance or risk management but also about using AI in a manner that sustains human development and social well-being.

If you consider the risks to which we could be exposed, this is even more important. Because AI can rapidly scale, it can amplify its benefits and harms, especially when one simple application can affect millions of lives within days or hours. This reach means that even ethical oversights have consequences. Both the negative and positive impacts can promote communities and create opportunities at an unimaginable scale. At the same time, using AI ethically is not about restricting innovation but ensuring its development moves in the right direction. When ethical considerations are prioritized, we are preventing problems and creating technology that better serves human needs. This approach leads to more sustainable, trustworthy, and successful AI implementations.

The challenge, in this case, is recognizing that ethical AI development is a path that must be trailed and adjusted along the way. As AI capabilities expand and society evolves, new ethical considerations are likely to appear. What seemed acceptable yesterday might raise eyebrows tomorrow. This dynamic requires us to maintain constant vigilance and adaptation to the current conditions, especially if we want to remain relevant in the market. It is also important to acknowledge that responsible AI is a collective responsibility. While individual developers and companies make specific decisions, the impact of these choices helps shape our future. Every choice we make regarding AI carries implications.

For AI technology users, ethical responsibility extends beyond all the companies and individuals who are developing the technology. As AI becomes more integrated into our lives, it is important to approach these tools with awareness and responsibility. This means understanding its limitations, verifying important information, and using these tools in ways that respect others' rights and privacy.

Users should be mindful of how they use AI-generated content, especially in professional and academic contexts. Maintaining transparency is essential, particularly when it affects others. Just as ethical frameworks were developed for other technologies, the same should be done regarding AI use. The shared responsibility between creators and users helps ensure that technology works positively in our society.

Finally, remember the impact that AI has already had on our lives. It is shaping our future and how we interact with one another. The ethical choices we make today will determine what it will be like in the future. Therefore, ethical AI is not the right thing, but the *best thing* to do. The commitment to ethical AI is more than just preventing harm. It is also about actively working to create a future in which humans and machines can work together.

HOW TO BE TRANSPARENT WITH AI PRACTICES

As you might imagine, transparency has become one of the most important elements in AI use and development, leading companies to create standards and countries to develop regulations. Although ethical implementations are guiding the way AI should be used, being transparent is essential to ensure that the technology remains accessible to others and that decisions can be explained. This transparency will allow us to communicate, implement, and maintain dialogue on these models and systems.

Transparency when using and developing AI systems requires a systematic approach regarding documentation and communication. However, this means more than just informing users that you are using the technology but also providing the necessary details so users can understand, question, and engage with it. To do this, you must ensure that the necessary documentation is available, and the decision-making process is clear. Additionally, stakeholders must be able to understand when the system is updated, and when there are changes, they can provide feedback when necessary.

Providing users with training and information allows you to have a transparent approach to AI systems and allows stakeholders to feel more trust in its use and development process. While this might seem like too much work to take on for the implementation of a program, the process should not be seen as a burden. It should be identified as an opportunity to build relationships with users and improve system performance.

Finally, remember that these protocols, documentation, and procedures should be updated, reviewed, and communicated regularly. This will allow your model to remain effective and relevant, creating a sustainable approach to AI development. When this process is carried out correctly, it becomes a competitive advantage, allowing for continuous improvement in AI implementations and increased customer loyalty.

FUTURE TRENDS: WHAT TO EXPECT NEXT?

As AI continues to evolve, it is only natural that you start to question yourself on what are the next trends and developments that will happen in the market. Some consider that we are going too fast, while others are working tirelessly to ensure the next big development is available soon. To understand where we are and where we are going next, you must remember what you read about in Chapter 1, about the different types of AI. By understanding where we are and what is expected from these machines, you can see the next phase of AI development more clearly, as well as its potential impacts on business and society.

Multimodal AI

Today, most of the AI models we have are limited to one function. Think about how ChatGPT works mostly with text or Dall·E with images. These are just two examples that can be named, but this is the situation for almost all AI applications. The idea is that in the future, these models will work with different types of information: text, images, audio, and video. When this happens, we will have reached what is called multimodal AI. Different from the other types of AI systems that will work with only one type of data, these AI models can simultaneously integrate and analyze different types of data, leading to a more nuanced understanding.

One example of this multimodal AI in action would be a system that can analyze a video conference by processing not only the spoken words, but also facial expressions, voice tone, and body language. If AI can have this capability, it will open up new opportunities in fields such as healthcare and education, allowing a more comprehensive understanding for professionals using the tools. In this multidimensional approach, AI would still be limited to understanding the data without becoming general AI, but it would increase human capability to better understand situations by using machine insight.

The Increasing Reach of LLMs

Throughout the book, you have seen the different ways that LLMs are being incorporated into different tools. You have seen how Google is adding Gemini to its suite, just as Microsoft is doing the same with its applications. This is the next step where LLMs are moving on from standalone tools into integrated components of larger systems. When this happens, the AI model will work with other tools such as databases and non-AI software, creating powerful and versatile systems that can handle complex tasks.

As these systems become more sophisticated, they will be able to understand the context and maintain long-term memory of their interactions. They will also get better at carrying out specialized tasks within their industries. Today, many of the solutions offered on the market are going in that direction, allowing companies and individuals to leverage AI for better outcomes.

Explainable AI

As you have already seen in the previous section, the concept of ethical and transparent AI is gaining momentum. As these programs become more complex and influential in our daily activities, it becomes essential to understand how the decisions are made. This explains the growth of explainable AI (xAI) as a field working to make AI systems more transparent, understandable, and interpretable to nontechnical stakeholders.

Currently, we have companies and individuals who have their content on the internet questioning how the information was collected and used, and even if there is authorization to do so. Lawsuits have been filed to ensure that content is not used to train AI systems, especially due to accountability. This movement is especially important in regulated industries like healthcare and finance, where decision transparency is often legally required.

Regulatory and Compliance Landscape

Speaking of regulation and compliance, the world is now seeing an increase in regulations and frameworks to govern AI. One of the pioneers in this implementation was the European Union, which published legislation in 2024 regarding how AI should and should not be used within its borders. Frameworks such as these aim to address concerns regarding privacy, fairness, transparency, and ethical use of these tools.

In the future, we are likely to see other countries following suit. There will be new data protection regulations, requirements for transparency, and standards for AI testing and validation. International cooperation among countries regarding AI use and development is also expected. Organizations such as the International Association of Privacy Professionals and others have created maps and trackers to identify how legislation and regulations are being developed and implemented as well as their current status.

Technology Democratization

One of the most discussed topics regarding AI is how the technology is reaching different people. While those with more financial power have access to the latest tools, others with limited budgets struggle to adopt the technology due to its cost. This offers large organizations and those who are wealthier access to models and AI programs that are not immediately available to smaller businesses and those with less money. While this was a reality in the past, the future seems to bring promising opportunities to democratize technology.

User-friendly tools and platforms are making it easier for individuals and small businesses to leverage AI capabilities that were once exclusive to large tech companies. This is leading to more accessible development tools and platforms, as well as lower costs for AI implementation. With more companies using the technology, there is increased competition and innovation, greater diversity in AI applications, and new opportunities for entrepreneurs like yourself, who consider using AI to make money.

Impact on Global Industries

Different markets are expected to see a significant impact with the increased use of AI. Traditional industries are being transformed, and new ones are being created. Manufacturing, for example, is becoming more automated and efficient through predictive maintenance and smart robotics. Healthcare is seeing advances in diagnosis and drug development. Financial services are being revolutionized by AI-driven analysis and personalized services.

However, it is not only these industries that will be impacted. This transformation also creates new job categories at the same pace as eliminating or changing others. Today, we have a growing demand for AI specialists and the evolution of traditional roles to incorporate AI skills. Professionals with human skills that complement AI are being highly valued in the market, leading to significant shifts in workforce distribution across industries.

In this new market, companies that incorporate professionals with AI knowledge will become more diverse and competitive. As large companies continue to drive innovations, we are expected to see the rise of specialized AI service providers and a growth in AI consulting and implementation services. You should also expect to see an increased development of industry-specific AI solutions and an increased focus on regional and local AI applications, designed to meet specific and targeted needs.

Those who want to remain relevant in the market must stay informed and adaptable to the changes to come. Those who leverage these advances in their personal and professional lives will be more valuable to the market, especially if they maintain ethical standards and ensure human values. The next few years are promising and exciting, but it is essential that we remain conscious and aware that it is our job to guide its development to ensure it is beneficial to society.

PREDICTIONS FOR AI IN THE NEXT DECADE

Looking into the future, it is likely that AI and technology will continue to shape the way we live. In the next ten years, it is probable we will have a convergence of technologies that will become more powerful and personalized. With the increased processing power and computer capabilities, you could say that we are on the brink of transformation. Here are some of the expectations for the next years regarding AI and how it will relate to other technologies:

- **Evolution of AI technology:** AI technology is expected to achieve new levels of sophistication, blurring the lines between machine and human knowledge. These systems are expected to develop a more nuanced understanding of content and cultural events and better reasoning capabilities and logical thinking. In addition, researchers are working to create programs that have improved emotional intelligence and empathy with an increased capacity to solve complex problems. As machines develop a greater capacity to think like humans, they are expected to have a deeper understanding of human behavior and motivations (*The AI Index Report*, 2024).
- **The Internet of Things (IoT) and AI integration:** With the increase of technologies such as IoT, billions of devices are expected to be connected to AI technologies, decreasing 30% in energy consumption in smart homes and increasing customer satisfaction numbers by 25% (Rawjani, 2023). This integration will also allow the system to learn from real-time data across different sources, optimizing systems at all levels. Additionally, we will be able to predict and prevent problems before they happen. Finally, we will be able to create more efficient and sustainable environments, allowing smart cities and homes to work for us.
- **Personalization and collaboration:** Throughout the next few years, we will see AI becoming more personalized according to user needs. This means we should see AI assistants that

learn and adopt personal preferences more than they do now, and see healthcare become personalized with targeted approaches and education tailored to individual learning styles. It is also expected to have work environments adjusting to personal productivity patterns and according to each industry.

- **Automation and workforce:** Research has shown that 70% of CEOs believe that AI will change how their companies work and that there will be significant automation in work processes (*Artificial Intelligence*, 2023). AI is expected to change how companies interact with customers and modify the shopping experience for most of them. High-volume tasks are expected to be automated, including communications and software development tasks. Furthermore, we will see new professions appear and increased collaboration between humans and AI technology, with humans providing the necessary creativity and emotional intelligence these machines do not have.

- **Societal expectations and challenges:** As AI becomes a more significant part of our lives, it is normal that more details and explanations on how these machines make decisions are required. This means companies are expected to generate more transparent and explainable AI systems, create better privacy protection and data control, and implement ethical standards for their use. The market is in constant change and the need for more fair and unbiased AI systems is growing, just as more human control in the decision-making and output processes. In the next decade, companies are expected to increase their investments in xAI to make the technology more transparent and accessible.

- **Need for governance:** While tech companies are working at maximum capacity to increase their AI capabilities, governments are struggling to keep up with the industry's pace. At the same time, several countries have already started taking the necessary steps to regulate the industry and ensure that these systems are not harmful to society. In the next decade, we are likely to see an increase in global AI governance frameworks and international standards for AI development. Expect to see new regulatory bodies, oversight mechanisms, and ethics boards for AI development.

Looking ahead, you can see that we are not going to witness just technological evolution but also how our relationships in almost all life aspects will be changed. The decisions we make and the skills that we will need to develop in the coming years will determine how we will succeed in this new reality and approach the job industry.

After all these considerations, you might be asking yourself, *How can I prepare for this AI-powered future?* This is one of the most important questions that should be asked right now. To help you understand the next steps and how to best prepare for this new reality, as we move on to the last chapter of this book, you will see a road map that will help you develop skills, knowledge, and a mindset to develop in an AI-driven world. Shall we get ready and start preparing for the future? If your answer is *yes*, read on!

YOUR PERSONAL ACTION PLAN
TO MASTER AI

Throughout this book, different concepts regarding AI were explored, including its transformative potential and how it can be used to enhance your daily activities. You learned about the differences between AI systems and the ethical considerations that must be taken into account regarding them. LLMs are reshaping businesses, creating new opportunities for entrepreneurs, and allowing companies to leverage their power to become more competitive. As AI becomes more accessible to smaller organizations, we will see an increased use of the technology in everyday activities.

This final chapter serves as your practical guide to implementing AI in your professional life. Regardless of whether you are looking to integrate AI into an existing business, create a new AI income source, or optimize your activities, with all the information you are about to see all these options are possible. The concepts you have explored throughout this book will now be transformed into actionable steps to help you leverage the technology and ensure you remain updated and current with new AI developments. You will see how to

- assess your current AI knowledge and identify opportunities for AI integration
- select the right AI tools and platforms for your specific needs
- develop a realistic implementation timeline
- create sustainable AI-powered income streams
- build the necessary skills and knowledge
- address potential challenges and obstacles

As you read each of these steps, keep in mind that you do not have to become a technical expert to work and achieve success with AI. As you have seen, the secret is to know how to effectively leverage tools and platforms via the technology while remaining ethical. By implementing these steps, you will find that even for those with minimal AI and LLM knowledge, they can achieve the best results, without the need for specific details. No matter what industry you work in and what your objectives are with AI, you will see how to achieve your goals with real-life examples. Let's take a look at how this can be done!

STEPS TO INTEGRATE AI INTO DIFFERENT LIFE AREAS

Actioning what you have seen throughout this book might seem overwhelming, but you should not feel that way! In this step-by-step section, you will see how you can enhance your personal and professional life using AI. To do this, instead of viewing AI as a complex technology, think of it as a powerful assistant ready to help you achieve goals more efficiently.

AI for Personal Development

To start off, think about how you currently learn new skills or manage information. Now, consider a project or an area that you want to improve and that you feel could benefit from AI interaction. If this project refers to a personal development area you want to enhance, follow these steps:

1. Choose a topic you want more information on.
2. Open your preferred LLM (such as ChatGPT, Claude, or Gemini).
3. Instead of asking board questions, be specific, such as, "Create a structured 30-day learning plan for [topic], breaking it down into daily 1-hour sessions."
4. Use the AI to generate practice exercises and provide feedback.
5. As for explanations when the concepts are not clear, such as, "Explain [concept] using analogies from [your field of interest]."

In this case, if you are learning Spanish, for example, you might prompt the machine with the following, "I am a beginner learning Spanish. Create a conversation scenario about ordering food, then play the role of a waiter while I practice as a customer. Correct my grammar and pronunciation guidelines as we go."

AI for Professional Enhancement

To use AI for professional enhancement, you might need a little more time. This is because you will need to track your activities and then identify which ones you can automate. You will need to start small, with one task at a time, and only move to the next one once you are satisfied with the automation for the first. To carry out this process, follow these steps:

1. Track your daily tasks for a week and write them down.
2. After one week, identify the repetitive tasks, which can include replying to emails, report writing, and data analysis, among others.
3. For each of the tasks you identify, ask yourself, *Can AI help me automate this?*
4. Select one of the tasks to start with the automation.
5. Once you are satisfied and fully grasp the automation process for this task, move on to the next one.

An example of this process would be to automate the emails you send out. In this case, you can create an AI prompt that says, "I need to write professional emails for these common situations [*list situations*]." Create templates that maintain a consistent tone while being adaptable to different recipients.

Business Integration Strategy

Entrepreneurs and business owners looking to implement AI into their organizations can also achieve the objective by following a strategy. In this case, since it might mean significantly disrupting how business is carried out, you might need a timeframe of approximately 30 days to ensure that critical operations are not negatively impacted. If this is your idea, here is a structured approach to leverage the power of AI technology into your company:

- **Week 1:** Create an assessment of your company's processes. List all the relevant tasks and identify those that are the most time-consuming. Evaluate the current systems and tools in use and see if any could use an enhancement.
- **Week 2:** Research AI tools for your specific needs. Shortlist the most interesting tools and those who can help you optimize your tasks. During this process, you should take advantage of those tools that offer free trials. After carrying out the tests, calculate the potential return on investment with its implementation.
- **Weeks 3 and 4:** Implement the new tools to one specific task. You should take the integration process slowly, ensuring that one process is taken care of at a time. This should be carried out simultaneously with training team members.
- **After implementation:** Monitor results with established KPIs and adjust as needed.

This action plan will allow you to gradually evaluate the impact of AI on your company's processes and help you effectively monitor them.

You should ensure that these processes are independently monitored and that the results are satisfactory, such as reducing costs or time to carry out an activity. Only when you have the expected results, should you move on to the next task, as you will have a better view of how AI can help you.

Creating Passive Income With AI

If you are interested in creating passive income using AI, this is certainly possible! You can use the practical approach you will see next to identify potential areas where you can create these opportunities and develop an automated side hustle. This process includes the following steps:

1. Identify your niche or the area in which you would like to work in. This means identifying the knowledge you have and that others might value, solutions AI programs can offer, or creating digital products.
2. Start small with a few cases, such as one product or service. You can test different options and AI applications to see how they develop and answer the requests you are making.
3. Use beta testers to see if your solution works or if any changes must be made. Having three to four potential customers who will use the product and obtaining feedback will be valuable to see if you need to modify anything.
4. After all changes are made, go live with the content. This could mean building a website or blog to deliver the content or offering your services to potential customers.
5. Market your initiative and ensure that it is working properly.
6. Refine and review results periodically to ensure there are no flaws in the process or the information.

These steps should take around one to six weeks, during which you will slowly implement each stage. In a simulated timeframe, this is what it would look like:

- **Weeks 1–2:** Research your target market, use AI to analyze competitor offerings, see where you can add value and be different, and create a prototype of your product or service.
- **Weeks 3–4:** Test your product or service with a small audience and gather feedback. Refine your offering so that it meets customer needs.
- **Weeks 5–6:** Develop your marketing strategy and create supporting materials. Launch your product and see how it performs in the market. Create relevant KPIs to monitor your product's performance and reach.
- **After launch:** Iterate and verify if the service or product is working. Ensure there are no deviations in the output process and that the results are acceptable.

As you implement these solutions, remember that you must carefully analyze what you are going to offer. In some cases, implementation might take more time, but it will be worthwhile if this means you are ethically developing your solution and that you are going step-by-step. In many cases, it is better to go slow than to revolutionize everything at once. So, start with one area, perfect your approach, and then expand to others.

TOOLS AND PLATFORMS

When searching for the best AI tool to use, you will find there are several options in the market. This means you will need to carry out at least some research to see if what the tool provides you with caters to your needs and meets expectations. Once again, before you sign up for any of these, you should take advantage of the trial period to ensure it really fulfills your needs. In many cases, some of the tools you will see in this section also offer a free version you can test and experiment with to evaluate performance.

Content Creation

- **ChatGPT:** Creates written content, from marketing copy to blog posts with humanlike understanding.
- **Jasper:** Specializes in generating marketing content and brand-specific messaging.
- **Midjourney:** Generates high-quality images and visual content from text descriptions.
- **Pictory:** Automatically converts long-form videos into short social media snippets.

Logistics

- **Lineal:** Optimizes delivery routes and predicts demand patterns for efficient distribution.
- **Flexport:** Automates shipping documentation and provides real-time cargo tracking.
- **6 River Systems:** Manages warehouse operations with collaborative robots and AI.
- **Shipwell:** Offers predictive analysis for freight management and carrier selection.

Customer Management

- **Zendesk AI:** Automatically handles customer queries and routes complex issues to human agents.
- **Persado:** Personalizes customer communications using emotional AI.
- **Gong.io:** Analyzes customer calls to provide insights and improve sales conversations.
- **Drift:** Provides conversational AI for website visitor engagement and lead qualification.

Sales and Marketing

- **Salesforce Einstein:** Predicts sales opportunities and automates customer relationship management tasks.
- **Mailchimp AI:** Optimizes email marketing campaigns and segment audiences.
- **Albert:** Manages digital advertising campaigns across multiple platforms.
- **Crayon:** Tracks competitors and automatically provides market intelligence.

Financial Management

- **Xero AI:** Automated bookkeeping and categorizes transactions.
- **Stripe Radar:** Detects fraudulent transactions using ML
- **Freshbooks AI:** Manages invoicing and expense tracking with smart automation.
- **Sage AI:** Predicts cash flow and provides financial forecasting.

HR and Recruitment

- **HiredScore:** Screens resumes and matches candidates to job requirements.
- **Pymetrics:** Assesses job candidates through AI-powered games and exercises.
- **BreezyHR:** Automates interview scheduling and candidate communication.
- **Ideal:** Screens and grades candidates while reducing hiring bias.

Project Management

- **Monday.ai:** Suggests task prioritization and resource allocation.
- **Asana Intelligence:** Predicts project bottlenecks and suggests workflow improvements.
- **ClickUp AI:** Automates task creation and provides workload management.
- **Wrike Analyze:** Offers predictive project analysis and risk assessments.

Data Analysis

- **Tableau AI:** Creates automated visual insights from complex datasets.
- **Power BI AI:** Generates natural language insights from business data.
- **ThoughtSpot:** Provides AI-driven search-based analytics.
- **DataRobot:** Automates the process of building and deploying ML models.

These are only some of the examples of tools you will find on the market. With some research, you will find other tools that might be suitable for your business. Remember, this process will require some time and attention until you find the best solution. If you work with more people in your company, you can ask them to help you test these tools to see if they meet their demands and needs, as well as ensure that what you want to implement is useful.

It is usually ideal to start with one or two tools in the areas where you face the most immediate challenges. After you understand their suitability and how they can be used, you can expand your AI implementation throughout other areas. Finally, consider that most of these tools can work together with others, creating a better integration process for your business. For example, content creation tools can provide information for marketing automation, while customer management AI can inform sales strategies and logistics planning.

BUSINESS CASE

In the final part of this book, you will look into a fictional brand business case to understand how AI can help you develop your own business. In this case, the LLM being used is ChatGPT. Although the outputs presented in this section are a copy of what the machine has prompted, please remember that the results may not be the same when you insert them into your computer.

Project: Creating a fashion brand.

Prompt 1: *Generate 3 innovative business ideas at the intersection of sustainability, fashion, and sharing economy. Include market potential and key differentiators.*

Output 1: This is the output provided by ChatGPT, without modifications:

---

1. Circular Fashion Rental Platform

Concept: A peer-to-peer fashion rental marketplace for sustainable and ethically produced clothing. Users can rent out high-quality pieces they own or rent items for special occasions, minimizing waste and promoting reusability.

Market Potential: The global online clothing rental market is expected to reach $4.4 billion by 2028, driven by eco-conscious millennials and Gen Z.

Key Differentiators:

- Focus exclusively on sustainable and ethically certified brands.

- AI-powered recommendations for styles based on user preferences and events.
- Carbon offset program to make rentals 100% carbon-neutral.

2. Upcycled Fashion Co-op

Concept: A platform where independent designers can collaboratively upcycle used garments and sell them as unique, eco-friendly pieces. Consumers can donate unwanted clothes and receive discounts on purchases.

Market Potential: Upcycling aligns with the $6 billion sustainable fashion market and appeals to eco-conscious consumers seeking one-of-a-kind designs.

Key Differentiators:

- Direct collaboration between donors and designers for personalized upcycled creations.
- Community-based model supporting local artisans.
- Subscription option for regular "upcycled drops" tailored to individual styles.

3. Sustainable Fashion Subscription Box

Concept: A subscription service that curates eco-friendly, ethically sourced wardrobe staples for customers, focusing on timeless, high-quality pieces. Customers can return items they no longer use for resale or recycling.

Market Potential: The subscription box market is projected to grow at a 20% CAGR by 2030, with sustainability-focused niches attracting loyal customer bases.

Key Differentiators:

- Transparency on brand sourcing and production practices.
- Items tailored to each customer's climate and lifestyle to reduce wardrobe clutter.
- Gamification: Reward points for recycling or referring friends.

3. Sustainable Fashion Subscription Box

Concept: A subscription service that curates eco-friendly, ethically sourced wardrobe staples for customers, focusing on timeless, high-quality pieces. Customers can return items they no longer use for resale or recycling.

Market Potential: The subscription box market is projected to grow at a 20% CAGR by 2030, with sustainability-focused niches attracting loyal customer bases.

Key Differentiators:

- Transparency on brand sourcing and production practices.
- Items tailored to each customer's climate and lifestyle to reduce wardrobe clutter.
- Gamification: Reward points for recycling or referring friends.

Prompt 2: *I like option number 1, on the circular fashion rental platform. Can you help me create 5 names for this brand?*

Output 2:

- **LoopWardrobe:** Emphasizing the circular economy, "LoopWardrobe" conveys the idea of sharing and reusing clothing within a continuous loop.
- **StyleCycle:** A catchy, easy-to-remember name that highlights sustainability and the recurring use of fashionable items.

- **ReFash:** Short for "Refashion," this sleek name represents giving clothes a new life while staying trendy.
- **EcoThread:** Combining "eco" for sustainability and "thread" for fashion, this name speaks to the platform's core mission of eco-conscious clothing.
- **GreenCloset:** A warm, relatable name that evokes the image of an environmentally friendly wardrobe ready to be shared.

Prompt 3: *Now help me create a tagline that goes with the name ReFash, which is the name I selected among the options.*

Output 3:

"ReFash: Where Style Meets Sustainability." It succinctly conveys the platform's mission of blending trendy fashion with eco-conscious practices.

If you'd like alternatives, here are a few more options:

- "ReFash: Renew. Rewear. Redefine."
- "ReFash: Fashion Forward, Planet Friendly."
- "ReFash: Share the Style, Save the Planet."
- "ReFash: Modern Style, Sustainable Choice."
- "ReFash: Fashion with a Future."

Prompt 4: *What are the best channels to promote this product and what kind of content should I create to attract more customers?*

Output 4:

Promoting **ReFash**, a circular fashion rental platform, requires leveraging channels and content that resonate with your eco-conscious and fashion-savvy audience. Here's a tailored plan:

Best Channels to Promote ReFash

1. **Instagram**
   - **Why:** Highly visual platform, ideal for showcasing fashion styles and sustainable living content.
   - **What to Share:** Short reels of styling tips, before-and-after transformations, and eco-friendly lifestyle posts. Partner with influencers passionate about sustainability and fashion.
2. **TikTok**
   - **Why:** Popular among younger demographics, known for driving trends.
   - **What to Share:** Quick, engaging videos like "Outfit of the Day" (OOTD) challenges, creative unboxing of rental items, or fun skits emphasizing sustainability.
3. **Pinterest**
   - **Why:** A go-to for inspiration in fashion and lifestyle.
   - **What to Share:** Curated boards with outfit ideas, sustainability tips, and rental fashion hacks.
4. **YouTube**
   - **Why:** Perfect for long-form storytelling and tutorials.
   - **What to Share:** Mini-documentaries on sustainability in fashion, customer testimonials, and styling tutorials using ReFash items.
5. **Email Marketing**
   - **Why:** Great for nurturing leads and encouraging repeat customers.
   - **What to Share:** Exclusive discounts, styling newsletters, and updates about new inventory or sustainability milestones.
6. **Sustainability and Fashion Blogs**
   - **Why:** Reach an audience already interested in your niche.
   - **What to Share:** Guest posts or sponsored content about circular fashion and the benefits of renting over buying.

7. **Local Community Events**
   - **Why:** Personal connections foster trust and loyalty.
   - **What to Do:** Host pop-up styling events or workshops on sustainable living.

Content Ideas to Attract Customers

1. **Educational Content**
   - Explain how circular fashion works and its environmental impact.
   - Create infographics showing how renting fashion reduces waste.
   - Share "Did You Know?" posts about the fashion industry's carbon footprint.
2. **User-Generated Content (UGC)**
   - Encourage customers to share photos of their rented outfits with a branded hashtag (e.g., #ReFashStyle).
   - Feature UGC on your social media channels and website.
3. **Storytelling**
   - Share the origin story of ReFash to build a connection.
   - Highlight the journey of an item on the platform, from listing to rental.
4. **Lifestyle Integration**
   - Create content that shows how rental fashion fits into everyday life, such as weddings, parties, or work events.
5. **Exclusive Offers and Challenges**
   - Offer discounts for first-time renters.
   - Run challenges like "1 Month, 10 Outfits: Sustainable Style with ReFash."
6. **Sustainability Progress Reports**
   - Regularly update followers on how much waste your platform has saved.
   - Share testimonials from users about how ReFash changed their perspective on fashion.

7. **Behind-the-Scenes**
   - Post videos showing how you clean and prepare clothes for the next rental.
   - Highlight your team's commitment to sustainability.
8. **Partnership Content**
   - Collaborate with eco-friendly brands, influencers, or stylists.
   - Co-create content that ties their products/services with your rentals.
9. **Interactive Content**
   - Host live Q&A sessions on Instagram or TikTok about sustainable fashion.
   - Use polls and quizzes to engage your audience (e.g., "What's Your Sustainable Style Personality?").
10. **Case Studies and Success Stories**
    - Showcase how customers used ReFash for special occasions and loved the experience.
    - Share data on how renting fashion helps reduce environmental impact.

Additional Tips

- Focus on authenticity. Consumers value transparency and genuine efforts toward sustainability.
- Tailor content for each channel while maintaining consistent branding.
- Use analytics tools to track performance and refine your strategy.

Would you like assistance developing a more detailed content calendar or marketing strategy?

As you can see, you will be able to refine the outputs and build on the previous prompt in the same conversation, allowing you to create a cohesive and all-around strategy for your business. The more prompts you add and the more feedback you provide to the program, the better it will become at understanding your needs and tailoring its responses. By iterating on the same project within the same prompt, it will be able to continue the conversation with context in the future.

CONCLUSION

"AI is the future." How many times have you heard a phrase like this in the middle of a discussion at work or between friends? The truth is that the technology has come to stay, even if its consequences and development in the future are still unknown. As it becomes more accessible and powerful, it presents early adopters with an opportunity to leverage its potential and create value in ways that were not possible a few years ago.

While some might still discuss the ethical ramifications the technology might have, such as job displacement and digital segregation, others are using this opportunity to create extraordinary things. If your condition fits the first, you are not wrong but missing out on being part of the change. As these applications continue to evolve and expand, it is up to those using them to ensure they foster an inclusive, ethical, and safe environment. Consider: *What better way than to do this by implementing AI thoughtfully and responsibly in your own ventures?*

With the information you have received and the road maps you have seen throughout this book, you can start using AI *right now* to change your business or your personal life. From understanding foundational concepts to ideas on how to create passive income, you can now see that the possibilities are endless, allowing you to make an impact in whichever area you choose. Use your creativity, determination, and commitment to ensure that you have the best options that align technology with ethical and transparent practices.

Finally, remember the tools you use are just *tools*, meaning you will need to bring your mindset and ideas to the table. AI is not a magical solution but a means and an enabler to help you make your ideas come true. To ensure you stay updated on the latest information on the market, follow technology blogs; new solutions are being presented daily, and it will be up to you not to stay behind!

To help you start working with these AI tools and practice prompting, you will see that following this conclusion, there is a *bonus chapter* with a few market prompts you can use to leverage LLMs. They have been crafted to help entrepreneurs and business owners inspire and provide practical ways to integrate AI into their business strategies. Use them to spark your creativity, refine business workflows, and discover innovative opportunities.

Yes, AI is the future, but the technology does not survive on its own. It is also about the people who use it and its impact. If you are ready to lead the way and change how business works, there is no better time to start than now! It is time to turn these ideas into income and be a part of the change, not just a spectator. It is now up to you: Are you prepared to change your life by leveraging AI?

BONUS CHAPTER: BUSINESS PROMPTS FOR EVERYDAY USE

The prompts you will see in this section were created for specific purposes and have placeholders for you to add your specific area. They have also been optimized by ChatGPT to bring you the best outcome, ensuring they are effective and deliver the expected results. You can use these prompts for your business or even to create a new income source. Feel free to modify them and change them according to your needs and demands! Remember that as you create and modify each prompt, you should provide the machine with some context to ensure it understands your needs.

EXISTING BUSINESSES

Here are a few prompts you can use if you have an existing business and want to optimize your operations using AI.

Marketing and Customer Engagement

- Write a [type of marketing copy] promoting a [product/service] that emphasizes [unique selling point]. The tone should appeal to [target audience].

- Create a content calendar for a [specific platform] for a [type of business] targeting [specific demographic] over the next [timeframe].
- Draft a [type of campaign] for a [type of business]. Include three key messages and a call-to-action to drive [specific result].
- Generate three tagline options for a [product/service] that convey [core value] to [target audience].
- Develop a creative strategy for a [type of ad] to attract [specific audience] and achieve [specific goal].

Product Design and Development

- Brainstorm ideas for a [type of product] that addresses [specific problem or trend]. The design should appeal to [target audience] and emphasize [specific features].
- Suggest five improvements for an existing [product/service] in a [specific industry] to meet the needs of [specific customer group].
- Draft a development roadmap for a [new product/service] targeting [specific market]. Include milestones for [specific phases].
- Propose three features for a [software, app, tool] that would differentiate it in the [specific market] and meet [specific user needs].
- Generate ideas for packaging a [type of product] that is [adjective] and aligns with [brand values].

Customer Service and Support

- Draft responses for frequently asked questions in [specific format] for a [type of business]. Prioritize clarity and helpfulness.
- Create a script for a [specific customer service scenario] in a [type of business] that ensures a positive customer experience.

- Design a chatbot flow for a [specific purpose] in a [type of industry]. The tone should be [adjective].
- Suggest ways to improve customer feedback collection for a [type of business]. Focus on [specific goals].
- Generate three personalized email templates for following up with [specific customer actions]. Emphasize [specific outcome].

Data Analysis and Reporting

- Analyze [specific dataset or metric] for a [type of business]. Identify trends and suggest actionable insights to improve [specific area].
- Generate a report outline for [specific performance metric] with key sections focusing on [specific aspects].
- Provide predictions for [specific trend or behavior] based on [type of historical data] to guide [specific decision].
- Suggest KPIs for tracking the success of a [specific initiative] in a [type of business].
- Draft a presentation summarizing the [specific analysis] for stakeholders, highlighting [specific focus areas].

HR and Team Development

- Develop an onboarding plan for [specific role] in a [type of business]. Include training modules and milestones for the first [timeframe].
- Create a job description for a [specific role] emphasizing [specific qualifications, skills, or company values].
- Generate three icebreaker activities for [specific event] in a [type of team].
- Suggest a performance review framework for evaluating [specific employee type] in a [type of organization]. Focus on [specific metrics].

- Draft a diversity and inclusion training agenda for employees in a [specific industry or company size]. Address [specific challenges].

Finance and Budgeting

- Create a monthly budget template for a [type of business] focused on [specific priorities].
- Generate financial projections for [specific initiative or new product] over the next [timeframe]. Include key assumptions.
- Propose cost-saving strategies for a [type of business] without compromising [specific goal].
- Draft a pitch deck slide explaining the ROI of investing in [specific product/service] for [specific audience].
- Create a financial risk assessment for [specific business decision].

Sustainability Initiatives

- Propose eco-friendly practices for a [type of business] to minimize [specific impact] and appeal to [specific customer segment].
- Develop a plan for achieving [specific sustainability certification] for a [type of project or business].
- Suggest ways to incorporate sustainability messaging into the branding of a [specific product/service].
- Create a green supply chain strategy for a [type of business] to meet [specific sustainability goals].
- Draft an internal sustainability report framework for [specific industry or company size].

DEVELOPING PASSIVE INCOME SOURCES

Use the prompts you will see in this section to help you create a passive income source and leverage LLMs to help you identify the strategy and the action plan for how it will be launched.

Content Creation

- Generate a list of [specific type of content] targeting [specific audience]. The content should focus on [specific niche] and be designed for [monetization method].
- Write a step-by-step guide on [specific topic] that is optimized for SEO, targeting [specific keywords] and aimed at [specific audience]. Include actionable tips and a call-to-action for [specific purpose].
- Create a week-long social media content calendar for [specific platform] focused on [specific topic or niche]. Include captions, hashtags, and post ideas for engagement.
- Draft a long-form article or e-book on [specific subject] aimed at [specific goal]. Provide sections that detail [specific subtopics].
- Generate ideas for a YouTube channel targeting [specific demographic] in the [specific industry/niche]. Suggest themes, episode formats, and monetization strategies.

Ecommerce and Dropshipping

- Create product descriptions and marketing copy for a [specific type of product] sold through a [specific platform]. Ensure the tone appeals to [target audience] and includes [specific features] to increase conversions.
- Identify trending products in [specific industry] that could perform well in a dropshipping business targeting [specific audience]. Provide potential suppliers and pricing strategies.

- Write an email marketing sequence to promote a flash sale for [specific product] on [specific platform]. Include subject lines and call-to-action phrases to maximize conversions.
- Generate ideas for bundling [specific types of products] to increase average order value. Suggest pricing and promotion strategies for [specific audience].
- Draft a compelling FAQ section for a product page selling [specific item], addressing common concerns like [specific issues].

Online Courses and Digital Products

- Outline the curriculum for an online course teaching [specific skill] aimed at [specific audience]. Include engaging lesson ideas, exercises, and potential upsell opportunities like [specific add-ons].
- Design an engaging webinar outline on [specific skill or subject] that serves as a lead magnet for an online course. Include key talking points and interactive elements.
- Create a sales page for a digital product, such as [specific type], targeting [specific audience]. Highlight benefits, testimonials, and a call-to-action.
- Generate email templates to promote an upcoming online course launch on [specific subject]. Include urgency tactics like early bird discounts.
- Outline a content strategy for a podcast aimed at promoting a digital product related to [specific niche]. Suggest episode themes and guest ideas.

AI-Powered Subscription Services

- Design an AI-powered subscription service for [specific use case]. List the key features and benefits that would appeal to [specific customer base] and outline a plan for pricing and scaling the service to generate recurring revenue.

- Develop a pricing strategy for an AI-powered subscription service in [specific field]. Suggest tiers and corresponding features for different customer segments.
- Create a landing page copy for an AI service offering [specific feature]. Focus on clear value propositions and customer testimonials.
- Draft a customer retention email series for a subscription service in [specific industry], aiming to reduce churn and improve engagement.
- Generate a list of partnership opportunities for a subscription service focused on [specific niche]. Suggest cross-promotions and cobranded campaigns.

Affiliate Marketing Automation

- Generate a series of automated email sequences promoting [specific affiliate products]. Each email should focus on [specific benefits] and include calls-to-action to drive traffic to [specific platform or website]. Tailor the tone to resonate with [specific audience].
- Write a script for a YouTube video promoting [specific affiliate product]. Focus on storytelling and how the product solves a common problem.
- Generate blog content ideas that naturally incorporate affiliate links for [specific type of product] aimed at [specific audience].
- Develop a social media campaign plan to promote affiliate products in [specific niche]. Include post themes and ad copy ideas.
- Draft an automated chatbot flow to recommend affiliate products based on user preferences in [specific industry].

NEW BUSINESS IDEAS

If you are looking to start a business, AI might help you find the ideal niche and customers for it! You can use the examples you will see below to develop a customized service based on your abilities and skills, allowing you to start something new or even a side hustle. Use and adapt the information below to become an entrepreneur.

Personalized Wellness Coach

- Design an AI-powered daily wellness program for [specific demographic]. Include features like meal planning, fitness tracking, and stress management tips.
- Generate a series of app notifications for a personalized wellness AI targeting [specific goal]. Ensure they are motivational and actionable.
- Draft a landing page for an AI wellness coach app, highlighting how it adapts to user behavior over time to deliver personalized results.
- Develop an onboarding sequence for new users of a wellness AI app, ensuring they set clear goals and understand key features.
- Create a content marketing strategy for a blog promoting an AI wellness coach, focused on [specific topic].

AI-Powered Language Tutoring

- Create a curriculum for an AI-powered language tutoring app for [specific language]. Include interactive lessons and real-time practice suggestions.
- Draft a social media campaign promoting an AI language tutor, targeting [specific audience].
- Write an FAQ section for a website offering AI-powered language lessons, addressing common concerns like [specific concerns].

- Generate a gamification strategy for an AI language learning app, incorporating rewards for milestones like [specific goals].
- Create a series of emails to engage and retain users of an AI-powered language tutoring service, focusing on their progress and achievements.

Sustainable AI-Powered Fashion Recommendations

- Generate a recommendation engine for sustainable fashion, suggesting [specific type of items] based on user preferences and eco-friendliness ratings.
- Draft a blog post about how AI is revolutionizing sustainable fashion, aimed at attracting environmentally conscious consumers.
- Write ad copy for a campaign promoting an AI-powered sustainable fashion platform, emphasizing [specific benefits].
- Create an email series targeting users of a sustainable fashion AI tool, highlighting new eco-friendly products and how they align with their preferences.
- Design an AI-powered style quiz for a sustainable fashion platform, helping users discover their style while focusing on eco-friendly options.

AI-Powered Virtual Interior Designer Assistant

- Create an AI-powered virtual interior design assistant that helps users redesign a room by suggesting furniture, color palettes, and layouts based on their style preferences and budget.
- Develop a system where users can upload photos of their rooms, and the AI recommends design changes, offering links to purchase suggested items.
- Generate marketing content for an AI interior design tool that targets first-time homeowners, offering them personalized design solutions and cost estimates.

- Write a blog post outlining the benefits of using an AI virtual interior design assistant, focusing on convenience, affordability, and time-saving features.
- Create a chatbot script that helps users choose the right furniture and decor based on their space size, personal preferences, and budget.

Custom Meal Planning and Recipe Service With AI

- Design an AI-powered meal planning service that generates custom weekly menus based on dietary preferences, nutritional needs, and available ingredients.
- Generate a subscription service for personalized AI meal plans, where users receive recipes and grocery shopping lists tailored to their taste and health goals.
- Create an AI chatbot that helps users find recipes based on what they currently have in their fridge or pantry, reducing food waste and offering alternatives.
- Write a content marketing strategy for a website promoting AI-driven meal plans and recipes, aimed at busy professionals and health-conscious individuals.
- Generate a targeted email campaign for an AI meal planning service, highlighting customer testimonials and showing how the service saves time and improves meal variety.

Digital Marketing Automation Service

- Develop an AI-powered marketing automation tool for small businesses that creates personalized email sequences, social media posts, and ad campaigns based on customer behavior.
- Create an AI system that can analyze customer data and automatically generate content and ad campaigns to boost engagement and conversion rates for ecommerce businesses.
- Design a system where users can input their business goals,

and the AI suggests the best marketing strategies, channels, and content ideas to implement.

- Write a tutorial for small business owners on how to use an AI-driven marketing automation tool to enhance customer engagement and boost sales.
- Develop a marketing campaign plan for an AI digital marketing service targeting small business owners, emphasizing ease of use, cost-effectiveness, and measurable results.

REFERENCES

AI in education market worth $32.27 billion by 2030. (2024, November). Grand View Research. https://www.grandviewresearch.com/press-release/global-artificial-intelligence-ai-education-market

The AI index report – Artificial intelligence index. (2024). Stanford University. https://aiindex.stanford.edu/report/

Anderson, M. (2024, September 24). *Almost all small businesses are using a software tool that is enabled by AI.* AP News. https://apnews.com/article/small-business-artificial-intelligence-productivity-f6fa7b2a1ce0a9f2e5b8b48670b3098a

Artemakis A. (2024, January 12). *Large language models (LLMs) and their impact on everyday technology.* LinkedIn. https://www.linkedin.com/pulse/large-language-models-llms-impact-everyday-technology-artemiou-84def/

Artificial intelligence. (2023). PwC. https://www.pwc.com/gx/en/issues/artificial-intelligence.html

Artificial intelligence statistics 2024 - AI facts & stats report. (2024). AIPRM. https://www.aiprm.com/ai-statistics/

Bodiroza, M. (2023, September 6). The power of AI: HubSpot's generative AI content tools and ChatSpot. *New Perspective.* https://www.npws.net/blog/hubspot-generative-ai-tools

Boyer, D. (2024, November 4). *Case studies: How SMEs are using AI to compete with big players.* Inside Small Business. https://insidesmallbusiness.com.au/people-hr/productivity/case-studies-how-smes-are-using-ai-to-compete-with-big-players

ChatGPT. (2024). OpenAI. https://openai.com/chatgpt/overview/

51 artificial intelligence statistics to know in 2024. (2024). DigitalOcean. https://www.digitalocean.com/resources/articles/artificial-intelligence-statistics

Gemini. (n.d.). Google DeepMind. https://deepmind.google/technologies/gemini/

Introducing Meta Llama 3: The most capable openly available LLM to date. (2024, April 18). Meta. https://ai.meta.com/blog/meta-llama-3/

Kavanagh, K. (2023, December 22). *How artificial intelligence is revolutionizing diagnosis in health care.* Infection Control Today. https://www.infectioncontroltoday.com/view/how-artificial-intelligence-is-revolutionizing-diagnosis-health-care

Khan, A. (2024, June 20). *Conversational AI unveils $11 billion savings, 28.5% growth, and 91% business adoption.* TDM. https://www.thedevmasters.com/ai/conversational-ai-unveils-11-billion-savings-28.5-growth-and-91-business-adoption

Khan, J. (2024, August 24). *91+ eye-opening generative AI facts and stats (2024).* Learning Revolution. https://www.learningrevolution.net/generative-ai-facts-and-stats/

Lin, B. (2025, January 6). *How are companies using AI agents? Here's a look at five early users of the bots.* The Wall Street Journal. https://www.wsj.com/articles/how-are-companies-using-ai-agents-heres-a-look-at-five-early-users-of-the-bots-26f87845

Linacre, R. (2024, December 29). *The emerging impact of LLMs on my productivity.* RobinLinacre. https://www.robinlinacre.com/two_years_of_llms/

Llama. (2024). Meta Llama. https://www.llama.com/

Matleena S., & Brian. (2024, December 16). *AI statistics and trends: New research for 2025.* Hostinger. https://www.hostinger.com/tutorials/ai-statistics

Meet Claude. (2024). Anthropic. https://www.anthropic.com/claude

Merchant, B. (2024, July 23). *AI is already taking jobs in the video game industry.* Wired. https://www.wired.com/story/ai-is-already-taking-jobs-in-the-video-game-indus try/

Ms. Byte Dev. (2024, November 28). The impact of large language models (LLM) on everyday technology. *Stackademic.* https://blog.stackademic.com/the-impact-of-large-language-models-llm-on-everyday-technology-be391f2f134d

ODSC - Open Data Science. (2023, March 31). *5 practical business use cases for large language models.* Medium. https://odsc.medium.com/5-practical-business-use-cases-for-large-language-models-7b21b0059554

Rangarajan, K. (2024, January 1). *The impact of LLMs on learning and education.* Medium. https://medium.com/@keshavarangarajan/the-impact-of-llms-on-learning-and-education-3cd2a8367c23

Rawjani, M. M. (2023, October 30). *AI and IoT integration: Synergy for the future.* Medium. https://medium.com/@muzammil.rawjani/ai-and-iot-integration-synergy-for-the-future-9115a1ec2caf

Research Graph. (2024, September 19). *What is Grok?* Medium. https://medium.com/@ researchgraph/what-is-grok-3fc13cd61397

Revolutionising the legal world: The breakneck speed and pinpoint accuracy of AI technology for law firms. (2022, November 5). V500 Systems. https://www.v500.com/ai-advantage-how-law-firms-are-boosting-efficiency/

The state of AI in early 2024: Gen AI adoption spikes and starts to generate value. (2024, May 30). QuantumBlack. https://www.mckinsey.com/capabilities/quantumblack/our-insights/the-state-of-ai

Thomas, D. (2021, October 28). *Facebook changes its name to Meta in major rebrand.* BBC News. https://www.bbc.com/news/technology-59083601

Tilzer, B. (2024, April 9). How Best Buy is using generative AI to create better customer experiences. *Google.* https://blog.google/products/google-cloud/google-generative-ai-best-buy/

12 hyper personalization statistics that demonstrate value. (2024, October 9). *Monetate.* https://monetate.com/resources/blog/12-hyper-personalization-statistics-that-demonstrate-value/

Understanding the impact of large language models (LLMs) on businesses: Evaluating uses and integrations. (2023, September 18). Gaper. https://gaper.io/impact-of-large-language-models-llms/

Uspenskyi, S. (2024, September 19). *Large language model statistics and numbers (2024).* Springsapps. https://springsapps.com/knowledge/large-language-model-statistics-and-numbers-2024

xAI: Understand the universe. (2025). X.ai. https://x.ai/

www.ingramcontent.com/pod-product-compliance
Lightning Source LLC
LaVergne TN
LVHW041212050326
832903LV00021B/587

* 9 7 9 8 3 0 9 8 3 3 4 5 0 *